VERGIL
AENEID VIII

G000091425

Edited with introduction & notes by
H. E. Gould and
J. L. Whiteley

Published by Bristol Classical Press
General Editor: John H. Betts

(by arrangement with Macmillan & Co. Ltd.)

CONTENTS

* * * * * * *

Cover Illustration: HERCULES AND CACUS (Roman Bronze Medallion of about A.D. 140.)

Printed in Great Britain
ISBN O-906515-39-4

First published by Macmillan & Co., reprinted (1979) by

Bristol Classical Press
Department of Classics
University of Bristol
Wills Memorial Building
Queens Road
BRISTOL BS8 1RJ

FOREWORD

This edition of Vergil, Book VIII, has been prepared on the same principles as previous volumes in the Modern School Classics series. That is to say, the editors, believing that the annotated classical texts of the past generation give too little practical help in translation, and yet at the same time have their commentaries overloaded with unnecessary information on points only remotely connected with the text, have sought to write notes of a type better suited to the requirements of the school boy or girl of to-day, who is quite likely to embark on the preparation of the books set for the General Certificate Examination, Ordinary Level, without having previously read any continuous Latin texts at all.

In these times such pupils will need a great deal of help which in the spacious days of classical teaching fifty and more years ago they were considered not to require, and they will need moreover that such help should at first be given repeatedly, until each difficulty of construction becomes familiar.

The editors, bearing in mind, as they have tried to do throughout, the difficulties experienced by present-day pupils in the study of a subject which once received a much more generous share of the time-table, hope that they have done something, in the present edition, to smooth their path.

H. E. G.
J. L. W.

London, 1952

PREFACE TO THE BRISTOL CLASSICAL PRESS EDITION

There has in recent years been such a glut of editions
of *Aeneid* VIII that some may wonder at the reprinting of this
one; but, while *they* all aim to satisfy the needs of the more
advanced student, this edition is intended for those coming
to the *Aeneid* early in their careers, particularly those preparing for O-Level examinations. It may, nonetheless, be useful to draw attention here, for the benefit of both teacher
and ambitious student, to the following editions: R. D. Williams,
Virgil, *Aeneid* VII - XII (London, 1973); C. J. Fordyce, P. Ver-
gili Maronis *Aeneidos* Libri VII - VIII (Oxford, 1977); P. T.
Eden, A Commentary on Virgil *Aeneid* VIII (Leiden, 1975). Further Bibliography appears on page 148.

For reasons of economy most of the illustrations which
appeared in the original version of this edition have been
omitted (with the exception of those which appear on the cover
and pp. 20, 49 and 50) and for the same reason the original
version's appendix of annotated passages from Livy, Ovid and
Horace has also been omitted. These passages dealt with as-
pects of the legends and history of Rome which are treated in
Aeneid VIII: Ovid's account of Cacus and Hercules (*Fasti* I,
493 - 536); Livy's treatment of the same story (I, 7); three
passages of Livy dealing with Romulus, Remus and the she-wolf
(I, 4), the Sabine·women (I, 9) and the sacred geese of the
Capitol (V, 47); Ovid's description of the Golden Age (*Amores*
III, 8.35 - 52); and Horace's *Ode* on Antony and Cleopatra (I, 37).

BRISTOL, 1979   J.H.B.

INTRODUCTION

Publius Vergilius Maro

Vergil was born on 15th October, 70 b.c., at Andes near Mantua in Cisalpine Gaul—the Lombardy plain. Andes is usually identified with the present Pietole, three miles from Mantua ; this identification, however, has been rejected by some modern scholars, who favour a site close to the existing towns of Carpendolo and Calvisano.

The poet's family seems to have been of some local importance, and his father, who owned and worked a farm, was able to give his son the ancient equivalent of a university education. Vergil studied at Cremona and Milan, and later went to Rome to complete his course in rhetoric and philosophy.

No doubt his father wished Vergil to make his way, as Cicero had done, by his eloquence, first in the law courts as a pleader, or barrister, and then in politics by standing as a candidate for the various magistracies which led ultimately to the consulship and a seat in the senate. Vergil's temperament, however, for he was shy, nervous, and awkward in society, was quite unsuited to such a career, and after a single appearance before a jury, he decided to devote his life to philosophy and poetry.

Vergil returned to his native district, where he began

to write his first important work, the Eclogues, or
Bucolics, ten poems, in semi-dramatic form, in which
the persons are imaginary shepherds and their loves.
This fashion of poetry, called ' pastoral ', was developed
by the Sicilian Greek Theocritus.   The Eclogues made
Vergil's reputation as a poet and gained the attention
of Maecenas, who at that time was the most trusted
adviser in home affairs of Octavian, heir and successor
of Julius Caesar, and destined shortly to become master
of the Greco-Roman world as the first Roman Emperor,
Augustus.

During this period of his life, in 41 B.C., Vergil was
one of the many landed proprietors who saw their
farms ruthlessly confiscated and allotted to demobilized
soldiers—a common event during those troubled years
of civil war which preceded the collapse of the Roman
Republic.   Fortunately for the poet, however, the fame
of the Eclogues and his friendship with Maecenas made
Vergil's position secure under the new régime, and
enabled him to devote the rest of his life to poetical
composition, free from all economic anxiety, at Naples
and Nola in Campania.

Thus, in or about 37 B.C., Vergil began his second
great work, the Georgics, a long poem, in four books,
which describes the Roman methods of farming, the
production of crops, of the vine and the olive, the
breeding of stock and the keeping of bees.   As we
know from Vergil himself that he was asked to write
on this subject by Maecenas, we may safely assume

that this poem was designed as propaganda for Augustus' 'new order' in Italy, and to reinforce that Emperor's attempts to revive Roman religion, Roman agriculture, and the simple but hardy virtues which had made Rome great.

The two thousand odd lines of the poem were written very slowly, the years 37–30 B.C. being devoted to their composition, and reveal the highest standard of pure craftsmanship yet reached in Latin poetry. Moreover, though his subject in this poem might seem unlikely to produce great poetry, Vergil found the theme so congenial to his nature that he overcame the many difficulties, and not only produced a valuable text-book for farmers, but also wrote some of the noblest poetry in the Latin language.

Soon after the completion of the Georgics, Vergil, now forty years of age, embarked, again no doubt at the instigation of his political patrons, upon his greatest and most ambitious work, the writing of an epic, i.e. heroic narrative poem, the Aeneid, which should rival Homer's Iliad and Odyssey, and honour the imperial achievements of the Roman race, glorify the Roman character and focus Roman national sentiment on Augustus as the man sent by destiny to bring peace, stability, and prosperity to the Greco-Roman world, which had been racked for so many years by civil war, fear and uncertainty.

The Aeneid occupied Vergil's whole attention for the remaining years of his life. In 19 B.C., after a journey

to the East, he fell ill on his return to Italy at Brundi-
sium. His health had never been robust, and realizing
that his end was near, he gave instructions that the
great epic, for which he had planned a three years'
revision, and of whose imperfections, as an intensely
self-critical artist, he was very conscious, should be
destroyed. This instruction, fortunately for literature,
was disregarded by the poet's literary executors.

The Aeneid is an epic poem in twelve books, and
tells how a Trojan prince, Aeneas, a survivor from the
sack of Troy by the Greeks, is directed by the gods to
seek a new home in Italy. In that land, after many
vicissitudes, he settles with his Trojan companions, and
it is from these colonists that the Romans liked to
believe that they were sprung. Into this legend Vergil
weaves a glorification of the family of Augustus, con-
necting the Julian clan, to which it belonged, with
Iulus, the son of Aeneas.

Criticism of the poem has always recognized its
superlative artistry, despite Vergil's own dissatisfaction
with its lack of final polish, and is unanimous in detect-
ing in Vergil's mind, and reflected by the poem, a
profound sensibility and sympathy with human
troubles, which are hardly paralleled in Latin literature. In so far as judgment has been adverse, it has
fastened on the character of the hero, Aeneas himself,
in whom the virtue of *pietas*, ' dutifulness ', whether
towards father, country or gods, is allowed prominence
at the expense of warmer and more human feelings.

The story of the epic, book by book, is as follows :

BOOK I.   Aeneas and his companions are driven by a storm aroused by Juno, implacable enemy of the Trojan race, towards the North African coast, where, thanks to the intervention of Neptune, most of the ships find shelter, their crews landing safely and making their way to Carthage. In this city, which has just been founded by Dido, a young widowed princess from Tyre, they are hospitably received by the queen, who, at a banquet, invites Aeneas to relate the story of his wanderings.

BOOK II.   The Trojan hero begins his narrative with the story of the final siege, capture, and sack of Troy. We hear of the treacherous Sinon, who feigns to be a deserter, persecuted by his Greek fellows, in order to gain entrance to the city, of the trick of the Wooden Horse, the cruel death of Laocoon and his sons, who sought to warn the Trojans of their approaching doom, the entry of the Greeks, their murder of King Priam, and the escape of Aeneas from the burning city with his aged father, Anchises, his young son, Iulus, known also as Ascanius, and the household gods. In the confusion his wife Creusa is lost, but later Aeneas meets her ghost and is told that he is destined to found a new kingdom in Italy.

BOOK III.   The narrative continues with the escape of Aeneas and his Trojan comrades from the mainland, and their voyage to various places in search of the ' promised land '—to Thrace, Delos, Crete, and finally to the West, by way of the Strophades Islands, and the coast of Epirus (Albania), where Aeneas is advised by Helenus to sail round Sicily, to make for the west coast of Italy, and there to consult a prophetess, the Sibyl, at Cumae, and to appease Juno. Aeneas does as Helenus suggests, and thus, after seven years' wandering over the Eastern Mediterranean, he arrives at the western end of Sicily, where he spends the winter. Aeneas concludes his narrative to the queen, his hostess, by recording the death in Sicily of his father, Anchises.

Book IV. Meanwhile Dido, who has been greatly attracted to Aeneas from the first owing to the influence of Venus, his mother, now falls more and more deeply in love with him. Shortly after his arrival at Carthage, Dido and Aeneas by the power of Juno and Venus, who from quite different motives favour such a development, become lovers. Jupiter, however, now intervenes, and warns Aeneas, through Mercury, that he must leave Africa at once and fulfil his destined task of founding a new realm in Italy. Realizing the strength of Dido's passion for him, he tries to depart secretly, but his intentions become known to her. Yet he remains unmoved by her entreaties, which turn in the end to words of scorn and hatred. As he sails away, Dido destroys herself.

BOOK V. Aeneas returns to western Sicily and there celebrates the anniversary of his father's death with funeral games.[1] During the latter, Juno persuades the Trojan women, weary as they are of their wanderings, to set fire to the ships, but a sudden rain-storm subdues the flames and only four are destroyed. The Trojans sail away from Sicily. On the voyage Palinurus, the helmsman, is overcome by sleep, and falling overboard, is drowned.

BOOK VI. In this, to many readers the finest book of the poem, Aeneas, having at last set foot on the coast of western Italy, visits the Sibyl of Cumae and receives from her directions for the visit he longs to pay to the underworld. Armed with the ' golden bough ', which alone can procure him access to the nether regions of Hades, he traverses the various quarters of that kingdom, and meets the spirit of his father, who parades for Aeneas the souls of all great Romans that are awaiting incarnation. [2] In this way Vergil is able to give his readers a kind of national cavalcade of all the great figures in Roman history from the earliest times down to his own day. Thus the pageant closes

---

[1] The elaborate account of these games, which occupies most of Book V, is no doubt due to the influence of Homer, who in the Iliad describes at great length the funeral games of the hero Patroclus.

[2] Note again Vergil's indebtedness to Homer. Odysseus, too, in Book XI of the Odyssey, is made to visit the underworld.

with the greatest figure of them all, the emperor Augustus.

The sixth book contains the famous lines (851–3), which epitomize the Roman's pride in the city's greatness as an imperial power :

> Tu regere imperio populos, Romane, memento ;
> Hae tibi erunt artes ; pacisque imponere morem,
> Parcere subiectis, et debellare superbos.

‘ Thou, O Roman, remember to rule the nations 'neath thy sway,
These shall be thine arts, to impose the laws of peace,
To spare the conquered and to chasten the proud in war.’

BOOK VII. Aeneas at last enters his promised land by the mouth of the river Tiber, the natural frontier between the districts of Latium, lying south of the river, and Etruria to the north. He is welcomed by Latinus, king of Latium, who sees in Aeneas the bride-groom for his daughter, Lavinia, for whom he has been advised by an oracle to find a foreign husband.

Turnus, however, chieftain of the neighbouring Rutuli, and worthiest of Lavinia's suitors, is enraged at the proposal of Latinus, and, supported by Amata, the latter's queen, arouses the Latins against the Trojans. The book closes with a magnificent catalogue of the Italian forces—another epic convention, originating in Homer's catalogue of the Greek ships in the Iliad, Book II.

BOOK VIII. The river god Tiberinus sends Aeneas to seek aid from a Greek, Evander, who has settled on the Palatine Hill in what is destined to be the future

Rome. Evander promises help and conducts Aeneas through the city, explaining the origin of various Roman sites and names. Venus persuades Vulcan, her husband, to make Aeneas a suit of armour and a shield,[1] on which are depicted in relief various events in the future history of Rome, down to the battle of Actium, 31 B.C., by which Vergil's patron Augustus gained undisputed sovereignty over the ancient world.

BOOK IX. While Aeneas is absent, Turnus makes an attempt, barely frustrated, to storm the Trojan camp by the Tiber, and is successful in setting fire to their ships. Nisus and Euryalus, two Trojans, endeavour to slip through the enemy lines in order to inform Aeneas of the critical situation. They slay some of the foe, but are eventually discovered and killed. The next day, when Turnus renews his assault, he succeeds in entering the camp, but is cut off, and only effects his escape by plunging into the Tiber.

BOOK X. A council of the gods is held in Olympus and Jupiter decides to leave the issue of the war to fate. Aeneas now wins the support of an Etruscan army which has revolted against the cruelties of the king, Mezentius, and joined by reinforcements from Evander under the leadership of the latter's son, Pallas, he returns to aid the hard-pressed Trojans. In the furious fighting Mezentius and his son Lausus are slain, but Turnus kills Pallas.

[1] Homer, too, in the Iliad, Book XVIII, describes at length a shield, that of the Greek hero Achilles.

BOOK XI.   A truce is arranged for the burial of the dead.   On the arrival of an embassy from the Latins, Aeneas offers to settle the issue with a single combat between himself and Turnus.   The Latins hold a council of war and determine to continue the struggle, but they are defeated a second time by the Trojans and their allies in spite of many deeds of valour, especially on the part of Camilla, a warrior maiden who is killed in the fighting.

BOOK XII.   Another truce is arranged, and Turnus agrees to accept Aeneas' challenge, despite the opposition of the queen Amata and his sister, Juturna.   The latter provokes the Latins to violate the truce.   In the ensuing struggle Aeneas is wounded, but is miraculously healed by his mother, the goddess Venus.   He returns to the fray, routs the Latins and Rutulians and eventually meets Turnus in single combat.   The Rutulian chieftain is wounded and rendered helpless

Aeneas is minded to spare him until he notices that he is wearing the belt of the dead Pallas, whereupon he slays him.

The Metre of the Poem

Most English verse consists of lines in which stressed syllables alternate with unstressed, as for example in the lines :

' The ploughman homeward plods his weary way,
And leaves the world to darkness and to me.'

Such verse is called *accentual*.

The principle of Greek and Latin verse is different. It is based on the rhythmical arrangement of long and short syllables, the long syllables taking twice as long to pronounce as the short. This system may be compared with music, long syllables corresponding to *crotchets* and short to *quavers*, one *crotchet* being equal to two *quavers*. This type of verse is called *quantitative*.

Just as, to appreciate the rhythm of English verse, you are taught to *scan*, i.e. to divide the lines into *feet* and mark the stress in each foot, so you must learn to scan Latin verse by a similar division into feet by marking the syllables long (–) or short (‿). Not only is it necessary to do this in order to understand the construction of the verse and the musical qualities of the poetry, but the ability to do so is a great help in translation, by making it possible to distinguish words alike in spelling but different in *quantity*, for example, *pŏpŭlŭs*, ' people ', from *pōpŭlŭs*, ' poplar tree ', and *mīsērĕ*, ' they sent ', from *mĭsĕrē*, ' pitifully '.

The verses of the Aeneid are called heroic hexa-meters. In this verse two kinds of feet, or bars, are found. One is the *dactyl*, a long syllable followed by two short syllables, the other, the *spondee*, two long syllables. Each line, or hexameter, contains six feet, the first four of which may be either dactyls or spondees, the fifth being almost always a dactyl and the sixth a spondee. In place of this sixth-foot spondee a trochee (- ◡) is allowable.

Thus the scheme of the hexameter is as follows :

	1	2	3	4	5	6
	- ◡ ◡	- ◡ ◡	- ◡ ◡	- ◡ ◡	- ◡ ◡	- -
or	- -	- -	- -	- -		- ◡

In the scansion of these lines, no account is taken of syllables at the close of words *ending* in a vowel or an *m*, if they are followed immediately by a word *commenc-ing* with a vowel or an *h*. Such a final syllable is said to be elided, ' struck out ', though it was more probably slurred in pronunciation. Thus in l. 3 of the present book,

> *utque acres concussit equos, utque impulit arma,*

the final *e* of *utque* is ignored on both occasions in scanning.

A long syllable is one that contains a vowel long by *nature*, or a diphthong ; or a vowel, naturally short,

that is long by *position*, i.e. is followed by two consonants.

A short syllable is one that contains a vowel short by
nature and ends either with no consonant, or with only
one.

The two consonants which have been mentioned as
having the effect of lengthening a syllable need not both
occur in the same word. Thus in l. 5, -*at* is long, though
the *a* is naturally short, because that *a* is followed by a
t and the *t* of *trepido*.

PROSODY

The following information about the quantity of
Latin syllables will be found useful.

A. Relating to all syllables.

All diphthongs are long, except before another
vowel.

B. Relating to final syllables.

1. Final *a* is usually short.

Except

    (*a*) in the abl. sg. of 1st decl. nouns, e.g. *mensā* ;

    (*b*) in the 2nd sg. imperative active of 1st conjuga-
        tion verbs, e.g. *amā* ;

    (*c*) in indeclinable words such as *intereā, frustrā*.

2. Final *e* is usually short.

Except

    (*a*) in the abl. sg. of 5th decl. nouns, e.g. *aciē* ;

    (*b*) in the 2nd sg. imperative active of 2nd conjuga-
        tion verbs, e.g. *monē* ;

(*c*) in adverbs formed from adjectives of the 1st
and 2nd declensions, e.g. *pulchrē*, from
pulcher, -chra, -chrum. (Note, however,
benĕ, malĕ.)

3. Final *i* is usually long.

Except in *mihi, tibi, sibi, ubi, ibi*, in which it may be
long or short, and in *quasi, nisi*.

4. Final *o* is usually long.

Except in *modo, duo, ego*.

5. Final *u* is always long.

C. Final syllables of words of more than one syllable,
ending in any single consonant other than *s*, are short.

Except

(*a*) *dispār* ;

(*b*) in the perfects *iīt* and *petiīt*.

D. 1. Final *as, os, es*, are long.

Except

(*a*) *compŏs, penĕs* ;

(*b*) in nominatives singular in *es* of 3rd declension
nouns (consonant stems) having genitive
singular in *-ĕtis, ĭtis, -idis* ; e.g. *segĕs, milĕs,
obsĕs*. (But not *pariēs, abiēs*.)

(*c*) In compounds of *es* (from *sum*), e.g. *abĕs,
prodĕs*.

2. Final *us* and *is* are short.

Except *ūs*

(*a*) in gen. sg., nom., voc. and acc. pl. of 4th decl.
nouns, e.g. *gradūs* ;

(*b*) in the nom. sg. of consonant stem 3rd decl.
nouns having gen. sg. with a long syllable
before the last, e.g. *tellūs* (*-ūris*), *palūs*
(*-ūdis*), *virtūs*, (*-ūtis*).

And except *īs*

(*c*) in dat. and abl. pl., e.g. *mensīs, dominīs, vinīs* ;

(*d*) in acc. pl. of 3rd decl. *-i* stems, e.g. *navīs, omnīs* ;

(*e*) in the 2nd sg. pres. of 4th conjugation verbs,
e.g. *audīs* ; and in *sīs*, and compounds of *sīs*,
as *possīs* ; and in *velīs, nolīs, malīs,* and *īs*
(from *eo*).

E. Quantity of syllables determined by position in the
same word.

1. A syllable ending with a vowel or diphthong,
immediately followed by a syllable beginning with a
vowel, or with *h* and a vowel, is short ; e.g. *vĭa, prăe-
ustus, trăhit.*

Except

(*a*) in the case of genitives in *ius*, e.g. *alīus, solīus,
utrīus.* (But note *illĭus.*)

(*b*) *e* preceding *i* in 5th decl. nouns, e.g. *diēi,* and *ēi*
(from *is*).

(*c*) the syllable *fī* in *fīo.* (But note *fĭeri, fĭerem,*
the *i* being short before *er.*)

2. A syllable containing a vowel immediately followed
by two consonants, or by *x* or *z*, which are really double
consonants (*cs* and *ds*) is long ; e.g. the second syllable
in *regent, auspex.*

Except if the two consonants are a combination of one of the following, *b, c, d, f, g, p, t*, with (following) *l* or *r*.

If a short vowel precedes such a combination the syllable is not necessarily long.

Finally, it must be remembered that these rules apply to Latin words only, and not to many Greek proper names which will be encountered in this book.

Let us see now if, with the information given above, we can scan one of the hexameters of this book. Looking at line 3, for example,

utque acres concussit equos utque impulit arma

(i) See first whether any syllable requires to be elided, i.e. not taken into account. In this line the final *e* of *utque* (twice) will be disregarded before the initial vowels of *acres* and *impulit*.

(ii) Mark long (–) all syllables whose long quantity can be determined by the rules given above.

ut res con, cus, ut, qu'im, ar

are all ' long syllables ' (by Rule E 2). So is *os* (by Rule D 1).

This now gives us

ūtqu(e) acrēs cōncūssit equōs ūtqu(e) īmpulit ārma

(iii) Mark short (⌣) all syllables whose short quantity can be determined by rule.

The *it* of *concussit* and *impulit* is short (by Rule C) and the final *a* of *arma* (by Rule B 1).

Thus we now have

ūtqu(e) ācrēs cōncŭssĭt equōs ūtqu(e) ĭmpŭlĭt ārmă

Generally speaking, it will be found that such an application of the rules of prosody will give enough syllables of known quantity to make it possible to scan the line completely.

To do this, work backwards from the end of the line because the pattern of the last two feet

$$(- \cup \cup \mid - - \text{ or } - \cup)$$

is constant.[1]

This gives us for these feet :

ĭmpŭlĭt | *ārmă*

Working backwards again we shall find that the fourth foot is a spondee, the third a dactyl, the second and first spondees.

Thus the whole line, divided into feet and with the quantities marked, is :

ūtqu(e) āc | *rēs cōn* | *cŭssĭt ĕ* | *quōs ūt* | *qu(e) ĭmpŭlĭt*

| *ārmă*

[1] Very occasionally a spondee is found in the 5th foot. See for example lines 54 and 679 in this book.

One thing remains to be done before the scansion is complete. It is a rule that, usually in the third foot, more rarely in the fourth, one word must end and another begin. This is called caesura or ' cutting '. If the break occurs after the first syllable of the foot, the caesura is said to be strong ; if, after the second, weak. In this line we obviously have a strong caesura in the third foot. The caesura is regularly marked in scansion by a pair of vertical lines.

Thus the scansion of the line, as completed, is

$$\bar{u}tqu(e) \ \bar{a}c \mid r\bar{e}s \ c\bar{o}n \mid c\bar{u}ss\breve{i}t \parallel \breve{e} \mid qu\bar{o}s \ \bar{u}t \mid qu(e) \ \bar{i}mp\breve{u}l\breve{i}t$$
$$\mid \bar{a}rm\breve{a}$$

You will find that with careful attention to the pronunciation of Latin words, you will gradually learn to scan by ear, without the necessity of applying for help to the rules of prosody. You should try to develop this power as early as possible.

Note that the scheme of the hexameter makes it elastic, and gives it variable length, as long as 17 or as short as 13 syllables. This makes possible such onoma-topoeic lines as l. 596 in the present book :

$$Qu\bar{a}dr\breve{u}p\breve{e}- \mid d\bar{a}nt\breve{e} \ p\breve{u}- \mid tr\bar{e}m \parallel s\breve{o}n\breve{i}- \mid t\bar{u} \ qu\breve{a}t\breve{i}t \mid \bar{u}ng\breve{u}l\breve{a} \mid$$
$$c\bar{a}mp\breve{u}m$$

(where the poet, describing the galloping of horses, imitates the sound of them). And as line 452 *īll(i) īn-* | *tēr sē-* | *sē* || *mūl-* | *tā vī* | *brăcchĭā* | *tōllūnt*

(where again sound is matched to sense, for the line describes the alternate blows upon an anvil delivered by two smiths).

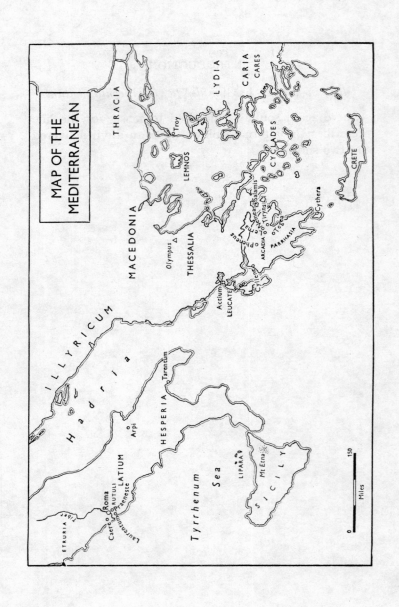

MAP OF THE
MEDITERRANEAN

ILLYRICUM

THRACIA

MACEDONIA

LYDIA

CARIA

CARES

Troy

LEMNOS

Olympus

THESSALIA

CYCLADES

CRETE

Actium
LEUCATE

Cyllene

Orpheus

Salamis

Mycenae

Tiryns

Enna

ARCADIA

Argos

PARRHASIA

Cythera

Hadria

Tarentum

HESPERIA

Arpi

ETRURIA

Tiber

Caere

Roma

RUTULI

LATIUM

Laurentum

Praeneste

Tyrrhenum
Sea

LIPARA

Mt Etna

SICILY

0   150

Miles

VERGIL
AENEID VIII

Throughout Latium the Rutulians and their allies prepare for war against the Trojans.

Ut belli signum Laurenti Turnus ab arce
extulit et rauco strepuerunt cornua cantu,
utque acres concussit equos, utque impulit arma,
extemplo turbati animi, simul omne tumultu
coniurat trepido Latium, saevitque iuventus   5
effera.   ductores primi Messapus et Ufens
contemptorque deum Mezentius undique cogunt
auxilia et latos vastant cultoribus agros.
mittitur et magni Venulus Diomedis ad urbem
qui petat auxilium, et Latio consistere Teucros,   10
advectum Aenean classi victosque penates
inferre et fatis regem se dicere posci,
edoceat, multasque viro se adiungere gentes
Dardanio, et late Latio increbrescere nomen :
quid struat his coeptis, quem, si fortuna sequatur, 15
eventum pugnae cupiat, manifestius ipsi
quam Turno regi aut regi apparere Latino.

Aeneas, harassed and careworn, receives comfort in a vision from the river god Tiberinus, who gives heartening prophecy and counsel.

Talia per Latium.   quae Laomedontius heros
cuncta videns magno curarum fluctuat aestu,

atque animum nunc huc celerem, nunc dividit illuc, 20
in partesque rapit varias perque omnia versat,
sicut aquae tremulum labris ubi lumen aenis
sole repercussum aut radiantis imagine lunae
omnia pervolitat late loca, iamque sub auras
erigitur summique ferit laquearia tecti. 25
nox erat et terras animalia fessa per omnes
alituum pecudumque genus sopor altus habebat,
cum pater in ripa gelidique sub aetheris axe
Aeneas, tristi turbatus pectora bello,
procubuit seramque dedit per membra quietem. 30
huic deus ipse loci fluvio Tiberinus amoeno
populeas inter senior se attollere frondes
visus (eum tenuis glauco velabat amictu
carbasus, et crines umbrosa tegebat harundo),
tum sic adfari et curas his demere dictis : 35
' O sate gente deum, Troianam ex hostibus urbem
qui revehis nobis aeternaque Pergama servas,
exspectate solo Laurenti arvisque Latinis,
hic tibi certa domus, certi (ne absiste) penates ;
neu belli terrere minis ; tumor omnis et irae 40
concessere deum.
iamque tibi, ne vana putes haec fingere somnum,
litoreis ingens inventa sub ilicibus sus,
triginta capitum fetus enixa iacebit,
alba, solo recubans, albi circum ubera nati. 45
[hic locus urbis erit, requies ea certa laborum.]
ex quo ter denis urbem redeuntibus annis
Ascanius clari condet cognominis Albam.

haud incerta cano. nunc qua ratione quod instat
expedias victor, paucis (adverte) docebo. 50
Arcades his oris, genus a Pallante profectum,
qui regem Evandrum comites, qui signa secuti,
delegere locum et posuere in montibus urbem
Pallantis proavi de nomine Pallanteum.
hi bellum adsidue ducunt cum gente Latina ; 55
hos castris adhibe socios et foedera iunge.
ipse ego te ripis et recto flumine ducam,
adversum remis superes subvectus ut amnem.
surge age, nate dea, primisque cadentibus astris
Iunoni fer rite preces, iramque minasque 60
supplicibus supera votis. mihi victor honorem
persolves. ego sum pleno quem flumine cernis
stringentem ripas et pinguia culta secantem,
caeruleus Thybris, caelo gratissimus amnis.
hic mihi magna domus, celsis caput urbibus exit !' 65

*As Aeneas, after grateful prayers to Tiberinus, is preparing for
his journey to Pallanteum, the God's prophecy is startlingly
fulfilled.*

　Dixit, deinde lacu fluvius se condidit alto,
ima petens ; nox Aenean somnusque reliquit.
surgit, et aetherii spectans orientia solis
lumina rite cavis undam de flumine palmis
sustinet, ac tales effundit ad aethera voces : 70
' nymphae, Laurentes nymphae, genus amnibus unde
　　est,
tuque, o Thybri tuo genitor cum flumine sancto,
accipite Aenean, et tandem arcete periclis.

quo te cumque lacus, miserantem incommoda nostra,
fonte tenet, quocumque solo pulcherrimus exis,   75
semper honore meo, semper celebrabere donis,
corniger Hesperidum fluvius regnator aquarum.
adsis o tantum et propius tua numina firmes.'
sic memorat, geminasque legit de classe biremes
remigioque aptat, socios simul instruit armis.   80
   Ecce autem subitum atque oculis mirabile monstrum.
candida per silvam cum fetu concolor albo
procubuit viridique in litore conspicitur sus :
quam pius Aeneas tibi enim, tibi, maxima Iuno,
mactat sacra ferens et cum grege sistit ad aram.   85
Thybris ea fluvium, quam longa est, nocte tumentem
leniit, et tacita refluens ita substitit unda,
mitis ut in morem stagni placidaeque paludis
sterneret aequor aquis, remo ut luctamen abesset.
ergo iter inceptum celerant. rumore secundo   90
labitur uncta vadis abies ; mirantur et undae,
miratur nemus insuetum fulgentia longe
scuta virum fluvio pictasque innare carinas.
olli remigio noctemque diemque fatigant,
et longos superant flexus, variisque teguntur   95
arboribus, viridesque secant placido aequore silvas.
sol medium caeli conscenderat igneus orbem,
cum muros arcemque procul ac rara domorum
tecta vident, quae nunc Romana potentia caelo
aequavit, tum res inopes Evandrus habebat.   100
ocius advertunt proras urbique propinquant.

*Alarmed at first at the approach of Aeneas with his Trojan galleys,
Evander and his people become friendly on learning who their
visitors are and why they have come. Aeneas asks Evander
to grant him an alliance, pleading that they are both sprung
from a common ancestor, Atlas.*

Forte die sollemnem illo rex Arcas honorem
Amphitryoniadae magno divisque ferebat
ante urbem in luco.   Pallas huic filius una,
una omnes iuvenum primi pauperque senatus   105
tura dabant, tepidusque cruor fumabat ad aras.
ut celsas videre rates atque inter opacum
adlabi nemus et tacitis incumbere remis,
terrentur visu subito, cunctique relictis
consurgunt mensis.   audax quos rumpere Pallas   110
sacra vetat raptoque volat telo obvius ipse,
et procul e tumulo : ' iuvenes, quae causa subegit
ignotas temptare vias? quo tenditis? ' inquit.
' qui genus? unde domo? pacemne huc fertis an
    arma? '
tum pater Aeneas puppi sic fatur ab alta,   115
paciferaeque manu ramum praetendit olivae :
' Troiugenas ac tela vides inimica Latinis,
quos illi bello profugos egere superbo.
Evandrum petimus.   ferte haec, et dicite lectos
Dardaniae venisse duces socia arma rogantes.'   120
obstipuit tanto percussus nomine Pallas :
' egredere o quicumque es,' ait, ' coramque parentem
adloquere, ac nostris succede penatibus hospes.'
excepitque manu, dextramque amplexus inhaesit.
progressi subeunt luco fluviumque relinquunt.   125

Tum regem Aeneas dictis adfatur amicis :
' optime Graiugenum, cui me Fortuna precari
et vitta comptos voluit praetendere ramos,
non equidem extimui, Danaum quod ductor et Arcas
quodque a stirpe fores geminis coniunctus Atridis ;   130
sed mea me virtus et sancta oracula divum,
cognatique patres, tua terris didita fama,
coniunxere tibi et fatis egere volentem.
Dardanus, Iliacae primus pater urbis et auctor,
Electra, ut Grai perhibent, Atlantide cretus,   135
advehitur Teucros ; Electram maximus Atlas
edidit, aetherios umero qui sustinet orbes.
vobis Mercurius pater est, quem candida Maia
Cyllenae gelido conceptum vertice fudit :
at Maiam, auditis si quicquam credimus, Atlas,   140
idem Atlas generat, caeli qui sidera tollit.
sic genus amborum scindit se sanguine ab uno.
his fretus non legatos neque prima per artem
temptamenta tui pepigi ; me, me ipse meumque
obieci caput et supplex ad limina veni.   145
gens eadem, quae te, crudeli Daunia bello
insequitur ; nos si pellant, nihil afore credunt,
quin omnem Hesperiam penitus sua sub iuga mittant,
et mare quod supra teneant, quodque adluit infra.
accipe daque fidem.   sunt nobis fortia bello   150
pectora, sunt animi et rebus spectata iuventus.'

Evander gives Aeneas a courteous and hospitable reply, and invites him and his comrades to partake of a sacrificial feast.

Dixerat Aeneas.   ille os oculosque loquentis
iamdudum et totum lustrabat lumine corpus.
tum sic pauca refert : ' ut te, fortissime Teucrum,
accipio agnoscoque libens!   ut verba parentis   155
et vocem Anchisae magni vultumque recordor!
nam memini Hesionae visentem regna sororis
Laomedontiaden Priamum, Salamina petentem,
protinus Arcadiae gelidos invisere fines.
tum mihi prima genas vestibat flore iuventas,   160
mirabarque duces Teucros, mirabar et ipsum
Laomedontiaden ; sed cunctis altior ibat
Anchises.   mihi mens iuvenali ardebat amore
compellare virum et dextrae coniungere dextram ;
accessi et cupidus Phenei sub moenia duxi.   165
ille mihi insignem pharetram Lyciasque sagittas
discedens chlamydemque auro dedit intertextam,
frenaque bina, meus quae nunc habet aurea Pallas.
ergo et quam petitis iuncta est mihi foedere dextra,
et, lux cum primum terris se crastina reddet,   170
auxilio laetos dimittam opibusque iuvabo.
interea sacra haec, quando huc venistis amici,
annua, quae differre nefas, celebrate faventes
nobiscum, et iam nunc sociorum adsuescite mensis.'

Haec ubi dicta, dapes iubet et sublata reponi   175
pocula gramineoque viros locat ipse sedili,
praecipuumque toro et villosi pelle leonis
accipit Aenean solioque invitat acerno.

tum lecti iuvenes certatim araeque sacerdos
viscera tosta ferunt taurorum, onerantque canistris 180
dona laboratae Cereris, Bacchumque ministrant.
vescitur Aeneas simul et Troiana iuventus
perpetui tergo bovis et lustralibus extis.

*Evander explains to his guests that this yearly sacrifice to the hero
Hercules is given in grateful memory of his destruction
of the monster Cacus, who for so long had preyed on the
inhabitants of the district.*

Postquam exempta fames et amor compressus
    edendi,
rex Evandrus ait : ' non haec sollemnia nobis,   185
has ex more dapes, hanc tanti numinis aram
vana superstitio veterumque ignara deorum
imposuit : saevis, hospes Troiane, periclis
servati facimus meritosque novamus honores.
iam primum saxis suspensam hanc aspice rupem,   190
disiectae procul ut moles, desertaque montis
stat domus, et scopuli ingentem traxere ruinam.
hic spelunca fuit, vasto summota recessu,
semihominis Caci facies quam dira tenebat,
solis inaccessam radiis ; semperque recenti   195
caede tepebat humus, foribusque adfixa superbis
ora virum tristi pendebant pallida tabo.
huic monstro Volcanus erat pater : illius atros
ore vomens ignes magna se mole ferebat.
attulit et nobis aliquando optantibus aetas   200

auxilium adventumque dei. nam maximus ultor,
tergemini nece Geryonae spoliisque superbus
Alcides aderat, taurosque hac victor agebat
ingentes, vallemque boves amnemque tenebant.
at furis Caci mens effera, ne quid inausum   205
aut intractatum scelerisve dolive fuisset,
quattuor a stabulis praestanti corpore tauros
avertit, totidem forma superante iuvencas.
atque hos, ne qua forent pedibus vestigia rectis,
cauda in speluncam tractos versisque viarum   210
indiciis raptos saxo occultabat opaco.
quaerenti nulla ad speluncam signa ferebant.
interea, cum iam stabulis saturata moveret
Amphitryoniades armenta abitumque pararet,
discessu mugire boves atque omne querelis   215
impleri nemus et colles clamore relinqui.
reddidit una boum vocem vastoque sub antro
mugiit et Caci spem custodita fefellit.
hic vero Alcidae furiis exarserat atro
felle dolor ; rapit arma manu nodisque gravatum   220
robur et aerii cursu petit ardua montis.
tum primum nostri Cacum videre timentem
turbatumque oculi ; fugit ilicet ocior euro
speluncamque petit ; pedibus timor addidit alas.
ut sese inclusit ruptisque immane catenis   225
deiecit saxum, ferro quod et arte paterna
pendebat, fultosque emuniit obice postes,
ecce furens animis aderat Tirynthius, omnemque
accessum lustrans huc ora ferebat et illuc,

dentibus infrendens.   ter totum fervidus ira   230
lustrat Aventini montem, ter saxea temptat
limina nequiquam, ter fessus valle resedit.
stabat acuta silex, praecisis undique saxis
speluncae dorso insurgens, altissima visu,
dirarum nidis domus opportuna volucrum.   235
hanc, ut prona iugo laevum incumbebat ad amnem,
dexter in adversum nitens concussit et imis
avulsam solvit radicibus, inde repente
impulit ; impulsu quo maximus intonat aether,
dissultant ripae refluitque exterritus amnis.   240
at specus et Caci detecta apparuit ingens
regia, et umbrosae penitus patuere cavernae,
non secus ac si qua penitus vi terra dehiscens
infernas reseret sedes et regna recludat
pallida, dis invisa, superque immane barathrum · 245
cernatur, trepidentque immisso lumine Manes.
ergo insperata deprensum in luce repente
inclusumque cavo saxo atque insueta rudentem
desuper Alcides telis premit, omniaque arma
advocat et ramis vastisque molaribus instat.   250
ille autem, neque enim fuga iam super ulla pericli,
faucibus ingentem fumum (mirabile dictu)
evomit involvitque domum caligine caeca,
prospectum eripiens oculis, glomeratque sub antro
fumiferam noctem commixtis igne tenebris.   255
non tulit Alcides animis, seque ipse per ignem
praecipiti iecit saltu, qua plurimus undam
fumus agit nebulaque ingens specus aestuat atra.

hic Cacum in tenebris incendia vana vomentem
corripit in nodum complexus, et angit inhaerens   260
elisos oculos et siccum sanguine guttur.
panditur extemplo foribus domus atra revulsis,
abstractaeque boves abiurataeque rapinae
caelo ostenduntur, pedibusque informe cadaver
protrahitur.   nequeunt expleri corda tuendo   265
terribiles oculos, vultum villosaque saetis
pectora semiferi atque exstinctos faucibus ignes.
ex illo celebratus honos, laetique minores
servavere diem, primusque Potitius auctor
et domus Herculei custos Pinaria sacri.   270
hanc aram luco statuit, quae maxima semper
dicetur nobis, et erit quae maxima semper.
quare agite, o iuvenes, tantarum in munere laudum
cingite fronde comas et pocula porgite dextris,
communemque vocate deum et date vina volentes.' 275
dixerat, Herculea bicolor cum populus umbra
velavitque comas foliisque innexa pependit,
et sacer implevit dextram scyphus.   ocius omnes
in mensam laeti libant divosque precantur.

*The sacrifice is renewed and hymns are
sung in honour of Hercules.*

Devexo interea propior fit Vesper Olympo.   280
iamque sacerdotes primusque Potitius ibant,
pellibus in morem cincti, flammasque ferebant.
instaurant epulas et mensae grata secundae
dona ferunt cumulantque oneratis lancibus aras.

tum Salii ad cantus incensa altaria circum   285
populeis adsunt evincti tempora ramis,
hic iuvenum chorus, ille senum, qui carmine laudes
Herculeas et facta ferunt : ut prima novercae
monstra manu geminosque premens eliserit angues,
ut bello egregias idem disiecerit urbes,   290
Troiamque Oechaliamque, ut duros mille labores
rege sub Eurystheo fatis Iunonis iniquae
pertulerit. 'tu nubigenas, invicte, bimembres,
Hylaeumque Pholumque, manu, tu Cresia mactas
prodigia et vastum Nemeae sub rupe leonem.   295
te Stygii tremuere lacus, te ianitor Orci
ossa super recubans antro semesa cruento ;
nec te ullae facies, non terruit ipse Typhoeus,
arduus arma tenens ; non te rationis egentem
Lernaeus turba capitum circumstetit anguis.   300
salve, vera Iovis proles, decus addite divis,
et nos et tua dexter adi pede sacra secundo.'
talia carminibus celebrant ; super omnia Caci
speluncam adiciunt, spirantemque ignibus ipsum.
consonat omne nemus strepitu collesque resultant.   305

*Evander, escorting Aeneas around his humble city, tells of the
     golden age of Saturn, and of his own arrival in Italy, and
     then introduces his guest to what is destined to be the site of
     the future Rome.*

   Exim se cuncti divinis rebus ad urbem
perfectis referunt.   ibat rex obsitus aevo,
et comitem Aenean iuxta natumque tenebat

ingrediens, varioque viam sermone levabat.
miratur facilesque oculos fert omnia circum   310
Aeneas, capiturque locis, et singula laetus
exquiritque auditque virum monimenta priorum.
tum rex Evandrus Romanae conditor arcis :
' haec nemora indigenae Fauni Nymphaeque tenebant,
gensque virum truncis et duro robore nata,   315
quis neque mos neque cultus erat, nec iungere tauros,
aut componere opes norant aut parcere parto,
sed rami atque asper victu venatus alebat.
primus ab aetherio venit Saturnus Olympo,
arma Iovis fugiens et regnis exsul ademptis.   320
is genus indocile ac dispersum montibus altis
composuit legesque dedit, Latiumque vocari
maluit, his quoniam latuisset tutus in oris.
aurea quae perhibent illo sub rege fuere
saecula : sic placida populos in pace regebat,   325
deterior donec paulatim ac decolor aetas
et belli rabies et amor successit habendi.
tum manus Ausonia et gentes venere Sicanae,
saepius et nomen posuit Saturnia tellus ;
tum reges asperque immani corpore Thybris,   330
a quo post Itali fluvium cognomine Thybrim
diximus : amisit verum vetus Albula nomen.
me pulsum patria pelagique extrema sequentem
Fortuna omnipotens et ineluctabile fatum
his posuere locis, matrisque egere tremenda   335
Carmentis Nymphae monita et deus auctor Apollo.'
    Vix ea dicta, dehinc progressus monstrat et aram

et Carmentalem Romani nomine portam
quam memorant, Nymphae priscum Carmentis
    honorem,
vatis fatidicae, cecinit quae prima futuros   340
Aeneadas magnos et nobile Pallanteum.
hinc lucum ingentem, quem Romulus acer asylum
rettulit, et gelida monstrat sub rupe Lupercal,
Parrhasio dictum Panos de more Lycaei.
nec non et sacri monstrat nemus Argileti,   345
testaturque locum, et letum docet hospitis Argi.
hinc ad Tarpeiam sedem et Capitolia ducit
aurea nunc, olim silvestribus horrida dumis.
iam tum religio pavidos terrebat agrestes
dira loci, iam tum silvam saxumque tremebant.   350
' hoc nemus, hunc,' inquit, ' frondoso vertice collem,
(quis deus incertum est) habitat deus ; Arcades ipsum
credunt se vidisse Iovem, cum saepe nigrantem
aegida concuteret dextra nimbosque cieret.
haec duo praeterea disiectis oppida muris,   355
reliquias veterumque vides monimenta virorum.
hanc Ianus pater, hanc Saturnus condidit arcem ;
Ianiculum huic, illi fuerat Saturnia nomen.'
talibus inter se dictis ad tecta subibant
pauperis Evandri, passimque armenta videbant   360
Romanoque foro et lautis mugire Carinis.
ut ventum ad sedes, ' haec,' inquit, ' limina victor
Alcides subiit, haec illum regia cepit.
aude, hospes, contemnere opes, et te quoque dignum
finge deo, rebusque veni non asper egenis.'   365

dixit, et angusti subter fastigia tecti
ingentem Aenean duxit stratisque locavit
effultum foliis et pelle Libystidis ursae :
nox ruit et fuscis tellurem amplectitur alis.

Venus, fearful for her son now that his foes are multiplied, begs
her husband Vulcan to make him armour and weapons for
the coming struggle. Vulcan accedes to her request and
descends to his forge beneath Mount Aetna.

At Venus, haud animo nequiquam exterrita mater, 370
Laurentumque minis et duro mota tumultu,
Volcanum adloquitur, thalamoque haec coniugis aureo
incipit et dictis divinum inspirat amorem :
' dum bello Argolici vastabant Pergama reges
debita casurasque inimicis ignibus arces,   375
non ullum auxilium miseris, non arma rogavi
artis opisque tuae ; nec te, carissime coniunx,
incassumve tuos volui exercere labores,
quamvis et Priami deberem plurima natis
et durum Aeneae flevissem saepe laborem.   380
nunc Iovis imperiis Rutulorum constitit oris :
ergo eadem supplex venio, et sanctum mihi numen
arma rogo, genetrix nato.   te filia Nerei,
te potuit lacrimis Tithonia flectere coniunx.
aspice qui coeant populi, quae moenia clausis   385
ferrum acuant portis in me excidiumque meorum.'
dixerat et niveis hinc atque hinc diva lacertis
cunctantem amplexu molli fovet.   ille repente
accepit solitam flammam, notusque medullas

intravit calor et labefacta per ossa cucurrit,   390
non secus atque olim, tonitru cum rupta corusco
ignea rima micans percurrit lumine nimbos.
sensit laeta dolis et formae conscia coniunx.
tum pater aeterno fatur devinctus amore :
' quid causas petis ex alto?   fiducia cessit   395
quo tibi, diva, mei?   similis si cura fuisset,
tum quoque fas nobis Teucros armare fuisset ;
nec pater omnipotens Troiam nec fata vetabant
stare decemque alios Priamum superesse per annos.
et nunc, si bellare paras atque haec tibi mens est,   400
quidquid in arte mea possum promittere curae,
quod fieri ferro liquidove potest electro,
quantum ignes animaeque valent, —absiste precando
viribus indubitare tuis.' ea verba locutus
optatos dedit amplexus, placidumque petivit   405
coniugis infusus gremio per membra soporem.
    Inde ubi prima quies medio iam noctis abactae
curriculo expulerat somnum, cum femina primum,
cui tolerare colo vitam tenuique Minerva
impositum, cinerem et sopitos suscitat ignes,   410
noctem addens operi, famulasque ad lumina longo
exercet penso, castum ut servare cubile
coniugis et possit parvos educere natos :
haud secus ignipotens nec tempore segnior illo
mollibus e stratis opera ad fabrilia surgit.   415
insula Sicanium iuxta latus Aeoliamque
erigitur Liparen, fumantibus ardua saxis,
quam subter specus et Cyclopum exesa caminis

antra Aetnaea tonant, validique incudibus ictus
auditi referunt gemitus, striduntque cavernis   420
stricturae Chalybum et fornacibus ignis anhelat,
Volcani domus et Volcania nomine tellus.
hoc tunc ignipotens caelo descendit ab alto.

The Cyclopes in their smithy are described, toiling at various
tasks : on the arrival of Vulcan to give them this new
commission, they set to work with fresh vigour to forge
arms for the Trojan hero.

Ferrum exercebant vasto Cyclopes in antro,
Brontesque Steropesque et nudus membra Pyracmon.
his informatum manibus iam parte polita   426
fulmen erat, toto genitor quae plurima caelo
deicit in terras, pars imperfecta manebat.
tres imbris torti radios, tres nubis aquosae
addiderant, rutili tres ignis et alitis Austri.   430
fulgores nunc terrificos sonitumque metumque
miscebant operi flammisque sequacibus iras.
parte alia Marti currumque rotasque volucres
instabant, quibus ille viros, quibus excitat urbes ;
aegidaque horriferam, turbatae Palladis arma,   435
certatim squamis serpentum auroque polibant,
conexosque angues ipsamque in pectore divae
Gorgona desecto vertentem lumina collo.
' tollite cuncta,' inquit, ' coeptosque auferte labores,
Aetnaei Cyclopes, et huc advertite mentem :   440
arma acri facienda viro.   nunc viribus usus,
nunc manibus rapidis, omni nunc arte magistra.

praecipitate moras.' nec plura effatus ; at illi
ocius incubuere omnes pariterque laborem
sortiti. fluit aes rivis aurique metallum,   445
vulnificusque chalybs vasta fornace liquescit.
ingentem clipeum informant, unum omnia contra
tela Latinorum, septenosque orbibus orbes
impediunt. alii ventosis follibus auras
accipiunt redduntque, alii stridentia tingunt   450
aera lacu. gemit impositis incudibus antrum.
illi inter sese multa vi bracchia tollunt
in numerum, versantque tenaci forcipe massam.

*The scene shifts back to Evander and his guest. It is next day
and the two heroes meet. Evander tells Aeneas how the
savage cruelty and tyrannical conduct of Mezentius, the
Etruscan king, have made his subjects revolt and expel him,
so that he has sought refuge with Turnus, the king of the
Rutuli. Evander suggests that Aeneas, the foreigner, is the
leader appointed by heaven to lead the Etruscan forces
wreaking vengeance upon their king. Moreover, Evander will
send his own son Pallas to the war under the protection of
Aeneas.*

Haec pater Aeoliis properat dum Lemnius oris,
Evandrum ex humili tecto lux suscitat alma   455
et matutini volucrum sub culmine cantus.
consurgit senior tunicaque inducitur artus
et Tyrrhena pedum circumdat vincula plantis.
tum lateri atque umeris Tegeaeum subligat ensem,
demissa ab laeva pantherae terga retorquens.   460
nec non et gemini custodes limine ab alto
praecedunt gressumque canes comitantur erilem.

hospitis Aeneae sedem et secreta petebat,
sermonum memor et promissi muneris heros.
nec minus Aeneas se matutinus agebat.   465
filius huic Pallas, illi comes ibat Achates.
congressi iungunt dextras, mediisque residunt
aedibus et licito tandem sermone fruuntur.
rex prior haec :
' maxime Teucrorum ductor, quo sospite numquam 470
res equidem Troiae victas aut regna fatebor,
nobis ad belli auxilium pro nomine tanto
exiguae vires : hinc Tusco claudimur amni,
hinc Rutulus premit et murum circumsonat armis.
sed tibi ego ingentes populos opulentaque regnis 475
iungere castra paro, quam fors inopina salutem
ostentat.   fatis huc te poscentibus adfers.
haud procul hinc saxo incolitur fundata vetusto
urbis Agyllinae sedes, ubi Lydia quondam
gens, bello praeclara, iugis insedit Etruscis.   480
hanc multos florentem annos rex deinde superbo
imperio et saevis tenuit Mezentius armis.
quid memorem infandas caedes, quid facta tyranni
effera?   di capiti ipsius generique reservent!
mortua quin etiam iungebat corpora vivis,   485
componens manibusque manus atque oribus ora,
tormenti genus, et sanie taboque fluentes
complexu in misero longa sic morte necabat.
at fessi tandem cives infanda furentem
armati circumsistunt ipsumque domumque,   490
obtruncant socios, ignem ad fastigia iactant.

VERGIL

ille inter caedem Rutulorum elapsus in agros
confugere et Turni defendier hospitis armis.
ergo omnis furiis surrexit Etruria iustis ;
regem ad supplicium praesenti Marte reposcunt.   495
his ego te, Aenea, ductorem milibus addam.
toto namque fremunt condensae litore puppes,
signaque ferre iubent, retinet longaevus haruspex
fata canens : " o Maeoniae delecta iuventus,
flos veterum virtusque virum, quos iustus in hostem 500
fert dolor et merita accendit Mezentius ira,
nulli fas Italo tantam subiungere gentem :
externos optate duces."   tum Etrusca resedit
hoc acies campo monitis exterrita divum.
ipse oratores ad me regnique coronam   505
cum sceptro misit mandatque insignia Tarcho,
succedam castris Tyrrhenaque regna capessam.
sed mihi tarda gelu saeclisque effeta senectus
invidet imperium seraeque ad fortia vires.
natum exhortarer, ni mixtus matre Sabella   510
hinc partem patriae traheret.   tu, cuius et annis
et generi fata indulgent, quem numina poscunt,
ingredere, o Teucrum atque Italum fortissime ductor.
hunc tibi praeterea, spes et solacia nostri,
Pallanta adiungam ; sub te tolerare magistro   515
militiam et grave Martis opus, tua cernere facta
adsuescat, primis et te miretur ab annis.
Arcadas huic equites bis centum, robora pubis
lecta dabo, totidemque suo tibi munere Pallas.'

Evander's words are confirmed by a sign from Venus, lightning and thunder in a cloudless sky. Aeneas joyfully recognises and accepts the portent of his divine mother. Aeneas and Pallas then make ready to depart.

Vix ea fatus erat, defixique ora tenebant   520
Aeneas Anchisiades et fidus Achates ;
multaque dura suo tristi cum corde putabant,
ni signum caelo Cytherea dedisset aperto.
namque improviso vibratus ab aethere fulgor
cum sonitu venit et ruere omnia visa repente,   525
Tyrrhenusque tubae mugire per aethera clangor.
suspiciunt, iterum atque iterum fragor increpat ingens.
arma inter nubem caeli in regione serena
per sudum rutilare vident et pulsa tonare.
obstipuere animis alii ; sed Troius heros   530
agnovit sonitum et divae promissa parentis.
tum memorat : ' ne vero, hospes, ne quaere profecto
quem casum portenta ferant : ego poscor. Olympo
hoc signum cecinit missuram diva creatrix,
si bellum ingrueret, Volcaniaque arma per auras   535
laturam auxilio.
heu quantae miseris caedes Laurentibus instant!
quas poenas mihi, Turne, dabis! quam multa sub undas
scuta virum galeasque et fortia corpora volves,
Thybri pater! poscant acies et foedera rumpant! '   540
    Haec ubi dicta dedit, solio se tollit ab alto,
et primum Herculeis sopitas ignibus aras
excitat, hesternumque larem parvosque penates
laetus adit ; mactat lectas de more bidentes
Evandrus pariter, pariter Troiana iuventus.   545

post hinc ad naves graditur sociosque revisit,
quorum de numero qui sese in bella sequantur
praestantes virtute legit ; pars cetera prona
fertur aqua segnisque secundo defluit amni,
nuntia ventura Ascanio rerumque patrisque.   550
dantur equi Teucris Tyrrhena petentibus arva ;
ducunt exsortem Aeneae, quem fulva leonis
pellis obit totum, praefulgens unguibus aureis.

*In words full of tender pathos, Evander regrets his lost youth and
prowess, and prays to the gods above to grant a safe return
to his son : and if that may not be, death for himself.   The
old man is completely overcome at the departure of his son.*

Fama volat parvam subito vulgata per urbem
ocius ire equites Tyrrheni ad limina regis.   555
vota metu duplicant matres, propiusque periclo
it timor, et maior Martis iam apparet imago.
tum pater Evandrus dextram complexus euntis
haeret inexpletus lacrimans ac talia fatur :
' o mihi praeteritos referat si Iuppiter annos,   560
qualis eram, cum primam aciem Praeneste sub ipsa
stravi scutorumque incendi victor acervos,
et regem hac Erulum dextra sub Tartara misi,
nascenti cui tres animas Feronia mater
(horrendum dictu) dederat, terna arma movenda   565
(ter leto sternendus erat ; cui tum tamen omnes
abstulit haec animas dextra, et totidem exuit armis) :
non ego nunc dulci amplexu divellerer usquam,
nate, tuo, neque finitimo Mezentius umquam
huic capiti insultans tot ferro saeva dedisset   570

funera, tam multis viduasset civibus urbem.
at vos, o superi, et divum tu maxime rector
Iuppiter, Arcadii, quaeso, miserescite regis
et patrias audite preces : si numina vestra
incolumem Pallanta mihi, si fata reservant,   575
si visurus eum vivo et venturus in unum :
vitam oro, patior quemvis durare laborem.
sin aliquem infandum casum, Fortuna, minaris,
nunc, nunc o liceat crudelem abrumpere vitam,
dum curae ambiguae, dum spes incerta futuri,   580
dum te, care puer, mea sola et sera voluptas,
complexu teneo, gravior neu nuntius aures
vulneret.'   haec genitor digressu dicta supremo
fundebat ; famuli conlapsum in tecta ferebant.

*Aeneas and his chosen warriors, together with the young Pallas,
leave to join the camp of Tarcho and the Etruscans.*

Iamque adeo exierat portis equitatus apertis   585
Aeneas inter primos et fidus Achates,
inde alii Troiae proceres, ipse agmine Pallas
in medio, chlamyde et pictis conspectus in armis,
qualis ubi Oceani perfusus Lucifer unda,
quem Venus ante alios astrorum diligit ignes,   590
extulit os sacrum caelo tenebrasque resolvit.
stant pavidae in muris matres oculisque sequuntur
pulveream nubem et fulgentes aere catervas.
olli per dumos, qua proxima meta viarum,
armati tendunt ; it clamor, et agmine facto   595
quadripedante putrem sonitu quatit ungula campum.

est ingens gelidum lucus prope Caeritis amnem,
religione patrum late sacer ; undique colles
inclusere cavi et nigra nemus abiete cingunt.
Silvano fama est veteres sacrasse Pelasgos,   600
arvorum pecorisque deo, lucumque diemque,
qui primi fines aliquando habuere Latinos.
haud procul hinc Tarcho et Tyrrheni tuta tenebant
castra locis, celsoque omnis de colle videri
iam poterat legio et latis tendebat in arvis.   605
huc pater Aeneas et bello lecta iuventus
succedunt, fessique et equos et corpora curant.

Venus appears to her son Aeneas, and presents to him the arms
wrought by Vulcan.

   At Venus aetherios inter dea candida nimbos
dona ferens aderat ; natumque in valle reducta
ut procul egelido secretum flumine vidit,   610
talibus adfata est dictis seque obtulit ultro :
' en perfecta mei promissa coniugis arte
munera : ne mox aut Laurentes, nate, superbos,
aut acrem dubites in proelia poscere Turnum.'
dixit, et amplexus nati Cytherea petivit,   615
arma sub adversa posuit radiantia quercu.
ille deae donis et tanto laetus honore
expleri nequit atque oculos per singula volvit,
miraturque interque manus et bracchia versat
terribilem cristis galeam flammasque vomentem,   620
fatiferumque ensem, loricam ex aere rigentem,
sanguineam, ingentem, qualis cum caerula nubes

solis inardescit radiis longeque refulget ;
tum leves ocreas electro auroque recocto,
hastamque et clipei non enarrabile textum.   625

A description of the shield, on which Vulcan has (prophetically)
   engraved important events from Roman history. Aeneas sees
   first the she-wolf that suckled the twins Romulus and Remus,
   then the rape of the Sabine women, the invader Porsenna,
   and a hero and heroine of the early Republic, Horatius who
   kept the bridge, and Cloelia.

Illic res Italas Romanorumque triumphos,
haud vatum ignarus venturique inscius aevi,
fecerat ignipotens, illic genus omne futurae
stirpis ab Ascanio, pugnataque in ordine bella.
fecerat et viridi fetam Mavortis in antro   630
procubuisse lupam, geminos huic ubera circum
ludere pendentes pueros et lambere matrem
impavidos, illam tereti cervice reflexa
mulcere alternos et corpora fingere lingua.
nec procul hinc Romam et raptas sine more Sabinas 635
consessu caveae, magnis Circensibus actis,
addiderat, subitoque novum consurgere bellum
Romulidis Tatioque seni Curibusque severis.
post idem inter se posito certamine reges
armati Iovis ante aram paterasque tenentes   640
stabant et caesa iungebant foedera porca.
haud procul inde citae Mettum in diversa quadrigae
distulerant (at tu dictis, Albane, maneres!),
raptabatque viri mendacis viscera Tullus
per silvam, et sparsi rorabant sanguine vepres.   645

nec non Tarquinium eiectum Porsenna iubebat
accipere, ingentique urbem obsidione premebat :
Aeneadae in ferrum pro libertate ruebant.
illum indignanti similem similemque minanti
aspiceres, pontem auderet quia vellere Cocles,   650
et fluvium vinclis innaret Cloelia ruptis.

Then follow the saving of the Roman citadel by the sacred geese,
the observances of the state religion, the punishment of the
traitor Catiline, and the reward of Cato, the patriot.

In summo custos Tarpeiae Manlius arcis
stabat pro templo et Capitolia celsa tenebat,
Romuleoque recens horrebat regia culmo.
atque hic auratis volitans argenteus anser   **655**
porticibus Gallos in limine adesse canebat ;
Galli per dumos aderant arcemque tenebant,
defensi tenebris et dono noctis opacae :
aurea caesaries ollis atque aurea vestis,
virgatis lucent sagulis, tum lactea colla   **660**
auro innectuntur, duo quisque Alpina coruscant
gaesa manu, scutis protecti corpora longis.
hic exsultantes Salios, nudosque Lupercos,
lanigerosque apices, et lapsa ancilia caelo
extuderat, castae ducebant sacra per urbem   **665**
pilentis matres in mollibus.   hinc procul addit
Tartareas etiam sedes, alta ostia Ditis,
et scelerum poenas, et te, Catilina, minaci
pendentem scopulo Furiarumque ora trementem,
secretosque pios, his dantem iura Catonem.   670

*The book closes with four notable scenes from the career of Augustus
the sea-fight off Actium, the flight of Cleopatra, the
triumph of Augustus in Rome, Augustus receiving the
gifts of the nation.*

Haec inter tumidi late maris ibat imago
aurea, sed fluctu spumabant caerula cano,
et circum argento clari delphines in orbem
aequora verrebant caudis aestumque secabant.
in medio classes aeratas, Actia bella, 675
cernere erat, totumque instructo Marte videres
fervere Leucaten auroque effulgere fluctus.
hinc Augustus agens Italos in proelia Caesar
cum patribus populoque, penatibus et magnis dis,
stans celsa in puppi, geminas cui tempora flammas 680
laeta vomunt patriumque aperitur vertice sidus.
parte alia ventis et dis Agrippa secundis
arduus agmen agens : cui, belli insigne superbum,
tempora navali fulgent rostrata corona.
hinc ope barbarica variisque Antonius armis, 685
victor ab Aurorae populis et litore rubro,
Aegyptum viresque Orientis et ultima secum
Bactra vehit, sequiturque (nefas!) Aegyptia coniunx.
una omnes ruere, ac totum spumare reductis
convulsum remis rostrisque tridentibus aequor. 690
alta petunt ; pelago credas innare revulsas
Cycladas, aut montes concurrere montibus altos,
tanta mole viri turritis puppibus instant.
stuppea flamma manu telisque volatile ferrum
spargitur, arva nova Neptunia caede rubescunt. 695

regina in mediis patrio vocat agmina sistro,
necdum etiam geminos a tergo respicit angues.
omnigenumque deum monstra et latrator Anubis
contra Neptunum et Venerem contraque Minervam
tela tenent.   saevit medio in certamine Mavors   700
caelatus ferro, tristesque ex aethere Dirae,
et scissa gaudens vadit Discordia palla,
quam cum sanguineo sequitur Bellona flagello.
Actius haec cernens arcum intendebat Apollo
desuper : omnis eo terrore Aegyptus et Indi,   705
omnis Arabs, omnes vertebant terga Sabaei.
ipsa videbatur ventis regina vocatis
vela dare et laxos iam iamque immittere funes.
illam inter caedes pallentem morte futura
fecerat ignipotens undis et Iapyge ferri,   710
contra autem magno maerentem corpore Nilum,
pandentemque sinus et tota veste vocantem
caeruleum in gremium latebrosaque flumina victos.
at Caesar, triplici invectus Romana triumpho
moenia, dis Italis votum immortale sacrabat,   715
maxima ter centum totam delubra per urbem.
laetitia ludisque viae plausuque fremebant ;
omnibus in templis matrum chorus, omnibus arae ;
ante aras terram caesi stravere iuvenci.
ipse, sedens niveo candentis limine Phoebi,   720
dona recognoscit populorum aptatque superbis
postibus ; incedunt victae longo ordine gentes,
quam variae linguis, habitu tam vestis et armis.
hic Nomadum genus, et discinctos Mulciber Afros,

hic Lelegas Carasque sagittiferosque Gelonos 725
finxerat ; Euphrates ibat iam mollior undis,
extremique hominum Morini, Rhenusque bicornis,
indomitique Dahae, et pontem indignatus Araxes.

*In wonder and delight at these pictures of a future he will not live
to see, Aeneas takes up the divine shield.*

Talia per clipeum Volcani, dona parentis,
miratur, rerumque ignarus imagine gaudet, 730
attollens umero famamque et fata nepotum.

HORATIUS COCLES.
(Roman bronze medallion of about A.D. 140)

THE WOLF AND THE TWINS.
(Silver coin of about 140 B.C.)

THE RAPE OF THE SABINES.
(Silver coin of about 87 B.C.)

ANTONY AND CLEOPATRA.
(Silver coin of about 36 B.C.)

THE VICTORY OF ACTIUM.
Bronze coin of about 10 B.C. in which the goddess Victory
is represented by Nicopolis, 'city of victory', founded
after Actium.

CLEOPATRA.
(Silver coin of about 40 B.C.)

AUGUSTUS' TRIUMPH IN EGYPT.
(Silver coin of 28 B.C.)

NOTES

Line 1. **ut** with the indicative means ' as ' or ' when '—the latter here.

belli signum, ' the signal for war '.

Laurenti is abl. sg. fem. of the adjective **Laurens** and in agreement with **arce,** ' from the Laurentian citadel '. The Laurentes were a Latin people who dwelt in Laurentum, a native city not far from the future Rome. Latinus was its king.

Turnus, king of the Rutulians, an Italian people, near neighbours of the Latins. See the epitome of the whole poem, given in the Introduction, for the part played by Turnus in the story. Book VII had ended with a catalogue of the forces which had come to the aid of Turnus.

l. 2. **cornua,** nom. pl.

l. 3. **ut,** ' when '. See note on l. 1.

concussit, ' he roused '.

impulit, ' he clashed '.

l. 4. **turbati** ; supply **sunt**. In prose and verse alike, parts of the verb **sum** are often omitted.

animi, nom. pl., ' their hearts '.

omne, in agreement with **Latium** in l. 5. Order for translation : **omne Latium coniurat trepido tumultu -que effera iuventus saevit.**

l. 6. **Messapus,** an ally of Turnus, is described in Bk. VII, l. 692, as invulnerable to fire and steel.

Ufens, another ally of Turnus.

l. 7. **Mezentius** is king of Caere in Etruria (north of the river Tiber). His aid has been sought by Turnus against Aeneas and his Trojans. In the latter half of the *Aeneid* in which he first appears, he is represented by Vergil as an impious man (**contemptor deum**) and as a tyrant.

51

deum. **-um,** the original form of the gen. pl. of the 2nd declension, is often found in poetry.

cogunt. With this verb take **primi;** 'first muster' ='are the first to muster'.

l. 8. **et latos . . . agros,** 'and strip the broad fields of husbandmen'. Note the abl. with **vastant** (separative).

l. 9. **mittitur et,** '(there) is sent, too'.

magni . . . ad urbem, 'to the city of mighty Diomedes'. The latter, a Greek, took part in the Trojan War, and afterwards, made his way to Italy where he founded Argyripa (Arpi) in Apulia.

l. 10. **qui petat.** Note the subj. mood, which expresses purpose here, 'to seek'.

ll. 10–14. **et Latio . . . nomen.** The key word in this sentence is **edoceat,** i.e. et qui edoceat, 'and to report'. Dependent upon this verb are three acc. and infin. clauses which precede, viz., **Teucros consistere Latio, Aenean advectum (esse) classi, -que inferre victos penates, (Aenean) dicere se posci fatis regem.** Two more follow, **multas gentes adiungere se Dardanio viro, et nomen increbrescere late Latio.**

l. 10. **Latio.** In poetry, 'place where' is often expressed by the abl. alone, without the preposition **in.**

l. 11. **Aenean advectum (esse),** 'that Aeneas had arrived'. Note the Greek form of the accusative sing. **victos penates,** 'his defeated household gods'. The **penates** were literally the gods of the store-cupboard. The phrase is the object of **inferre.**

l. 12. **et fatis . . . posci,** 'and that he (Aeneas) was saying that he was demanded by destiny (as) king'.

l. 14. **Dardanio** ='Trojan', Dardanus being an ancestor of Priam.

ll. 15–17. **quid . . . Latino.** In this sentence, which is still in indirect speech, the two indirect questions **quid . . . coeptis, quem . . . cupiat,** are subjects of the verb **apparere.**

'(they state that) what he (i.e. Aeneas) plans . . ., what issue of the fighting he hopes for if . . . appears more clearly to himself (**ipsi**) than to King Turnus or to . . .'

Note also : **quem** is an interrogative adj. with **eventum.**

l. 18. **talia** : supply **geruntur** or some verb of similar meaning : ' such things are being done throughout L. ' or ' such is the stir throughout L.'.

quae. The Romans liked to begin new sentences with relatives, where we prefer demonstratives. The antecedent to such relatives is usually in the preceding clause. Therefore render **quae** as **ea,** with **cuncta,** ' all these things '.

Laomedontius = ' Trojan '. Laomedon was a legendary founder of Troy.

l. 19. **magno** . . . **aestu,** ' tosses in a great surge of cares '.

ll. 20, 21. **atque** . . . **versat,** ' and now here, now there, he divides his nimble mind and hurries (it) in divers directions and turns (it) every way '. These two lines are repeated from Bk. IV, 285–6.

ll. 22, 23. **sicut** . . . **loca ;** order for translation : **sicut ubi aenis labris tremulum lumen aquae repercussum sole aut imagine radiantis lunae pervolitat late omnia loca.**

aenis labris, abl. of place where without preposition, ' in brazen bowls '.

pervolitat . . . loca, lit. ' flits far and wide over all the place ', i.e. ' darts here and there in all directions '.

l. 24. **sub auras,** lit. ' up to the breezes ', i.e. ' aloft ', ' on high '.

l. 25. **erigitur.** In Latin, the passive is often used as the equivalent of the active and reflexive pronoun ; thus **erigitur,** lit. ' is raised ', = ' raises itself '. This in turn corresponds to an English intransitive, here ' rises ' or ' climbs '.

summi tecti, ' of the roof above '.

l. 26. **animalia fessa,** acc., as is **genus** in the next line.

l. 27. **alituum** is an alternative form for **alitum** (from **ales**).

l. 28. **cum,** ' when '.

l. 29. **turbatus pectora,** ' disturbed in his heart ' ; **pectora,** acc. of respect and plural for singular.

l. 30. **seramque . . . quietem,** ' and allowed **(dedit)** sleep (though) late (to steal) over his limbs '.

l. 31. **fluvio Tiberinus amoeno,** ' Tiberinus of the pleasant river ', is in apposition with the subject **deus ipse,** as is **senior** in the next line. The latter has no comparative force, ' an aged figure '. Note **fluvio amoeno,** abl. of description.

l. 32. **se attollere,** ' to raise himself ' = ' to rise '. The reflexive is the equivalent of the English intransitive verb. Cf. the note on l. 25. The infinitive depends upon **visus** = **visus est,** ' appeared ', or ' seemed '.

l. 35. **adfari, demere,** are historic infinitives, i.e. they are to be translated as past indicatives. The subject is **Tiberinus.**

l. 36. **sate,** voc. sg. masc. of **satus,** perf. part. pass. of sero, lit. ' sown ', ' begotten ', i.e. ' son of '. It is followed by **gente** an abl. of origin. Aeneas was said to be the son of a mortal, Anchises; and of the goddess of love, Venus.

l. 37. **aeterna.** The adj. is used to express the result of the verb (a use known as proleptic), ' dost preserve Troy for ever '. **Pergama** is neut. pl.

l. 38. **exspectate,** voc. sg. masc. of the perf. part. pass. ' O thou, awaited '.

solo . . . Latinis, local abl. without preposition, ' on the . . .'

l. 39. **hic** is an adverb. Supply **est** as the verb.

ne absiste. In verse, **ne** with the imperative is often found where in prose we should have **noli** + infinitive.

penates, lit. ' household gods ', is often used for ' hearth ', ' home '.

l. 40. **neu** introduces a second negative command with **terrere** which is 2nd sg. imperative pass.

tumor omnis et irae, ' all the swelling and wrath ' = ' all the swelling wrath '. The figure of speech in which two nouns are found joined by a conjunction where we might expect one noun and an adjective, is known as hendiadys (lit. ' one through two ').

l. 41. **concessere** = concesserunt.   The alternative form -**ēre** for -**ērunt** in the perf. indic. act. is very common in the dactylic hexameter for metrical reasons.

The unfinished line reminds us that Vergil died before he had time to revise his epic.

l. 42. **iamque.**   After the first word, take the **ne** clause next, lit. ' lest thou should think that sleep fashions these vain (things).'   Translate ' these to be the vain imagining of sleep '.

tibi is dat. of the agent, a use of the case which is found in verse with the perfect passive, here **inventa.**

l. 43. **litoreis** : order for construing : **ingens sus inventa tibi iacebit** (l. 44) **sub litoreis ilicibus** . . .   Translate, however, ' thou shalt find a huge sow lying. . . .'

l 44. **triginta** . . . **enixa,** ' having brought forth a litter of thirty heads '.   **fetus,** pl. for sg.   For the use of **caput,** ' head ', cf. the English expression, ' thirty head of cattle '.

l. 45. **solo,** ' on the ground ', local abl.   **alba, albi,** would remind the Roman reader of Alba Longa, a town founded by Ascanius, the son of Aeneas, thirty years later.

l. 46. **laborum,** gen. dependent on **requies,** but to be translated as ' from thy labours '.   This gen. in Latin gives us the object of action implied in nouns or adjs.   English uses a preposition such as ' of ', ' for ', ' to ' or ' from '.

Note the Latin idiom by which the demonstrative pronouns **hic, ea** are attracted into the gender of the complementary nouns **locus, requies** as if they were demonstrative adjs.

This line is omitted by some of the best manuscripts : hence the brackets.   It may be genuine, however, because it occurs in the prophecy of Helenus which Vergil is repeating almost verbatim from III, 389 sqq.

l. 47. **ex quo** sc. **tempore,** ' after that time ', or if we understand **loco,** ' from this place '.   For **qui** = ' this ' or ' that ', see the note on l. 18.

ter denis . . . annis, 'within thrice ten years', abl. of time within which.   **denis**, lit. 'ten each', is poetical for **decem**.

clari cognominis (gen. of description), describes **Albam**.

l. 49. **haud incerta**, object of **cano**, 'most certain prophecies I utter'. 'Not doubtful' = 'very certain'. This figure of speech is called litotes.

ll. 49, 50. **nunc . . . docebo :** order for translation : **nunc docebo paucis verbis (adverte), qua ratione** ('by what means') **expedias victor quod instat.**

victor, adj. for adv., 'triumphantly' ; **quod instat**, 'what (i.e. the crisis which) threatens (thee)'.

l. 51. **his oris**, local abl., to be taken with **delegere** (53).

genus . . . profectum, 'a race sprung from P.', is in apposition with **Arcades**. The latter came from Arcadia, a district in the north of the Peloponnese (Greece).

l. 52. **Evandrum**, a descendant of the Arcadian hero, Pallas.

comites, '(as) companions'.   **secuti** = **secuti sunt**.

l. 53. **delegere.** See the note on l. 41.

l. 54. **Pallantis . . . Pallanteum**, '(named) Pallanteum, from the name of their ancestor Pallas'.

It seems probable that Evander was originally a minor deity, associated with Pan and worshipped in Arcadia. Legend, however, gave him a human origin and told how he left his native Arcadia to reach Italy, landing on the left bank of the Tiber and planting a settlement at what was to be the site of the future Rome on the Palatium, or Palatine Hill. Livy (I. 5) says 'the hill was called Pallantium from Pallanteum, a city of Arcadia, and then the Palatium hill'.

Cf. also Ovid, *Fasti*, V, 91 :

> exsul ab Arcadia Latios Evander in agros
> venerat impositos attuleratque deos.

l. 55. **ducunt**, 'prolong' or 'continue'.

l. 56. **socios**, '(as) allies'.

l. 57. **ripis . . . flumine**, 'along my banks and right up my stream', abl. of route.

l. 58. **adversum . . . amnem.** Begin with **ut** and render **sub-vectus** as a finite verb ' ascend ', inserting ' and ' before **superes.** The passive of **veho** and its compounds is often used as a deponent verb in the meaning of ' go ', ' ride ', ' sail ', etc.

adversum amnem, ' the river against thee '.

l. 59. **age.** The imperative of **ago,** when found with a second imperative, is translated ' come '.

nate dea, ' o goddess-born '. Cf. **sate gente deum,** l. 36.

primis . . . astris, abl. absol., ' when first the stars are setting '.

l. 60. **Iunoni.** Juno had always been the enemy of the Trojans ever since Paris, a Trojan prince, had decided against her in the dispute between the three goddesses, Juno, Venus and Minerva as to who was fairest. It was, therefore, essential for Aeneas to placate her.

l. 61. **victor,** ' after thy triumph '. **honorem,** ' worship '. Tiberinus will claim his due when Aeneas has emerged victorious.

l. 62. **ego sum.** The complement is **caeruleus Thybris** and should be translated next, i.e. before the **quem** clause.

caeruleus. The Romans were very vague in their use of colour adjectives and applied this one to the sky, the sea, rivers, serpents, olive trees and horses. It is mostly translated ' dark blue ', but is very unsuitable for the yellow and muddy Tiber.

l. 65. **hic . . . exit,** ' here (shall be) my stately home ; my source rises among lofty cities '. The **magna domus** is the future Rome. The Tiber rises in Etruria.[1]

l. 66. **lacu alto,** abl. of place where (local) without a preposition, ' in the deep pool '.

l. 67. **ima,** acc. pl. neut., ' the depths '. **Aenean:** the ending **-n** is that of the acc. sg., Greek 1st declension.

ll. 68–70. **surgit . . . sustinet :** order for translation, **surgit et spectans orientia lumina solis aetherii** ('in-the-heavens ') **sustinet rite undam de flumine cavis palmis.**

[1] Some translate : ' here rises (shall rise) my stately home, the head over proud cities '.

l. 70. **tales voces**, ' such words (as these) '.

aethera has a Greek acc. ending (3rd declension).

l. 71. **genus . . . est,** ' whence (=from whom) there is origin to streams ', = ' from whom streams have their origin '. The nymphs were the naiads of the springs.

l. 72. **Thybri,** voc. of **Thybris.**

l. 73. **tandem,** when found with an imperative, answers to ' I beg ', or ' I pray '.

ll. 74, 5. **quo te . . . exis,** ' in whatever spring the deep water (**lacus**) holds thee, pitying our woes, on whatever soil thou goest forth, in all thy beauty (**pulcherrimus**) '.

l. 76. **honore meo,** ' with sacrifices from me '.

celebrabere, note the ending -**re,** of the 2nd person sg. of the passive voice, which is often found in Latin verse.

l. 77. **corniger . . . aquarum,** ' (as) the horned river, ruler of the waters of Italy '.

fluvius may be taken as above, in apposition with the unexpressed subject of **celebrabere,** or as nom. for vocative. Rivers were often represented in ancient art with the head or horns of a bull, probably to symbolize their force and occasional violence.

Hesperidum : to the Greeks Italy was known as **Hesperia,** ' the land of the Evening ', i.e. the West. **Hesperidum** is gen. pl. of the adj. **Hesperis.**

l. 78. **adsis o . . . firmes,** 'only aid (us) and by thy nearer presence confirm thy will '.

Note : (i) **adsis, firmes,** jussive subj. in the 2nd person where we normally have the imperative. (ii) **numina,** pl. for sg.

l. 79. **geminas biremes,** ' two ships '. **biremis** is literally a ship with two banks of oars : actually it was not developed until long after the time of Aeneas. Vergil uses the word merely as a synonym for **navis.**

l. 80. **remigio.** Vergil uses the abstract ' rowing ' where we should say ' rowers '.

l. 81. **ecce ... monstrum.** In early Latin **ecce** ' behold ' was followed by an acc. case : Vergil may be imitating this idiom here or using an acc. of exclamation. The sense is the same : ' behold, however, a portent, sudden and wonderful to our sight (**oculis**) '.

ll. 81–3. **candida ... sus :** in translation keep the order of the Latin, ' (gleaming) white through the wood, of the same colour as her white litter (**fetu**), and lying upon the green bank is seen a sow '. **procubuit** is a finite verb, lit. ' there has lain down ', rendered here by a participle to throw the emphasis upon the last two words in the line, **conspicitur sus.**

l. 84. **quam,** ' it '. See the note on l. 18.

pius. pietas, the quality of right dealing as a son, a citizen, and a creature, for which in English we have three different expressions, filial dutifulness, patriotism, and piety, is the great virtue of Aeneas.

enim here means ' even '—a sense it has in earlier Latin— and emphasises the repetition of **tibi.**

l. 85. **sacra,** acc. pl. neut., ' the sacred vessels '.

cum grege, ' with her litter '. **ad,** ' at ' or ' before '.

l. 86. **ea, quam longa est, nocte** =totam eam noctem, ' all that night long '.

fluvium, ' flood '.

l. 87. **refluens,** ' checking his flow '. **substitit,** ' he stood still '.

l. 88. **in morem,** ' after the fashion ' : the genitives depend upon **morem.**

-que here =-ve, ' or '.

l. 89. **sterneret,** consecutive subj. ' (that) he levelled ', =' he made smooth '. **aequor aquis,** ' his watery expanse '. **aquis** is descriptive of **aequor,** and the latter is used of any level stretch, water, sea, plain or land.

remo . . . abesset, a purpose clause, ' that struggle might be absent for the oar ', =' that the rowers might not have to struggle '.

l. 90. **rumore secundo,** ' with cheerful cry ' or ' with heartening cheer '.

l. 91. **uncta,** from **ungo. vadis,** local abl. =**per vada.**

abies, lit. ' fir-wood ' =' the boat made of fir-wood ', or just ' the boat '. Cf. the English use of ' the steel ', for the weapon made of steel.

l. 92. **nemus insuetum,** nom., ' the grove unaccustomed (to the sight) ', =' the grove in great surprise '.

l. 93. **virum,** gen. pl. Cf. the note on l. 7.

fluvio . . . carinas. The **-que** seems to be misplaced. Begin with it, ' and the painted ships floating on the stream '.

fluvio, local abl. **pictas,** from **pingo. carina,** lit. ' keel ', is often used in poetry for ' boat ' or ' ship '—a figure known as synecdoche (part for the whole).

l. 94. **olli** =**illi. olle** is an old form of **ille.**

-que . . . -que, ' both . . . and '.

l. 95. **superant,** ' pass '. **teguntur,** ' are overshadowed '.

l. 96. **secant,** ' cut the green woods ', i.e. ' sail between the wooded banks '.

l. 97. **sol,** etc. It is now mid-day.

l. 98. **cum,** ' when ', introduces what is in effect, though not in grammar, the main clause of the sentence. In such cases (called ' inverse **cum** clauses ') the indicative is used, even with past tenses. **vident** in l. 99 is a historic present.

procul. The final syllable, naturally short, is lengthened by its position as the first syllable of the 4th foot.

l. 100. **tum . . . habebat.** Repeat **quae** from the previous line, ' (which) at that time (**tum**) Evander possessed, a tiny realm (**res inopes**) '. This translation emphasises that **res inopes** is in apposition with **quae,** object of **habebat.**

l. 102. **rex Arcas,** ' the Arcadian king ', is Evander.

sollemnem honorem, ' the wonted sacrifice '.

l. 103. **Amphitryoniadae magno**, ' to mighty Hercules's
Although the latter's father was said to be Zeus, Amphitryon
was his mother's husband and, therefore, the Greek hero is
often referred to by the patronymic Amphitryoniades, i.e. ' son
of A. '.

ferebat, ' was offering '.

l. 104. **Pallas ... una** ; supply **aderat**, ' his son Pallas was
with him '. **huic** dat. is to be taken closely with the adverb
una.

l. 105. **primi**, ' leading men '. **iuvenum**, ' of the warriors '.
iuvenis denotes a man of military age, i.e. from 18–45 years
old. **senatus** : naturally Vergil does not hesitate to use the
Roman term for the elders of Pallanteum.

l. 106. **tura**, pl. for sg.

l. 107. **ut**. See the note on l. 1.

videre = **viderunt**. This verb has first the object **celsas rates**,
then dependent upon it two acc. and infin., **(rates) adlabi**,
(viros) incumbere. ' When they saw the lofty ships and that
they were gliding between the shady groves and that the crews
were leaning on their silent oars.'

The picture becomes clear if we envisage the crews now resting
on their motionless oars as their ships glide to the bank.

l. 110. **quos**, ' them ' : the coordinating relative once again.
See the note on l. 18.

l. 111. **sacra**, ' the sacrifice '. **obvius**, ' to meet (them) '.

l. 112. **iuvenes**. Cf. the note on l. 105.

subegit : supply **vos** as the object.

l. 113. **quo**, ' whither ', ' where ... to '.

l. 114. **qui ... domo** ', lit. ' who (are you) as to race, whence
(are you) from home? ' i.e. ' of what race, are you, and
where is the home from which you come? ' **genus**, acc. of
respect.

arma, ' war ', **huc**, ' hither ', = ' here '.

l. 115. **pater Aeneas.** Aeneas is called father because to the Romans he was the father of their race.

l. 118. **illi,** ' the enemy ', i.e. ' the Latins '. **quos:** the antecedent is **Troiugenas,** l. 117.

profugos egere, ' have driven from their land '. **profugos,** proleptic, for which see l. 37, note.

l. 119. **ferte haec,** ' report these (words) '. **lectos,** ' chosen ', with **duces** in the next line.

l. 120. **socia arma,** ' allied arms '=' an alliance in arms ', i.e. ' in war '.

l. 121. **nomine** refers to the name of **Dardania** (Troy).

l. 122. **egredere** and **adloquere** need to be parsed carefully. If you remember that they come from deponent verbs, you will see that they are imperatives (2nd sing.). **coram** is an adverb, ' face to face '. **parentem** is the object of **adloquere.**

l. 123. **hospes,** ' (as) a guest '. **penatibus,** dat. with **succede,** ' enter '. For the meaning of **penates** see the note on l. 39.

l. 124. **amplexus inhaesit,** lit. ' having clasped, he clung to ', would be better as two finite verbs in English, ' he clasped and . . .' When in Latin a subject does, or suffers, two actions, it is very common to express the first of them by a participle. Cf. also the next line.

l. 125. **progressi.** The perfect participle of deponent verbs often has a *present* meaning.

luco would probably be **in lucum** in prose.

l. 127. **optime Graiugenum,** ' o noblest of the Greeks '. **Graiugenum,** gen. pl. See the note on l. 7. Here, however, -**um** replaces -**arum,** for **Graiugena** is 1st declension.

cui goes both with **precari** and **praetendere** in the next line. With **precor** the normal construction is acc. of the direct object.

l. 128. **vitta,** abl., as the scansion shows. It was customary to wreathe olive branches with woollen bands when making supplication. **comptos,** perf. part. pass. of **como.**

l. 129. **quod,** ' because '. **Danaum,** gen. pl. depending upon

ductor. With the latter and with **Arcas,** the verb **fores** (=esses) has to be supplied from the next line.

l. 130. **quodque . . . Atridis,** 'and because thou wast allied by birth to the two Atridae '.

The Atridae are the brothers Agamemnon, king of Mycenae, and Menelaus, king of Sparta and Helen's husband, who led the Greek expedition against Troy. Their father was Atreus ; hence they are frequently referred to by his name, and called the Atridae or ' sons of Atreus '.

fores is subj. because it is in virtual oratio obliqua. In other words, Aeneas is reporting some of his own thoughts.

ll. 131–3. **sed mea . . . volentem.** The verbs **coniunxere** and **egere** have four subjects and one object, **me,** with which **volentem** agrees.

It might be helpful in translation to begin with the object, ' but as for me, my merit . . .' and repeat it again after the first verb.

divum, gen. pl. again. **cognati patres,** lit. ' our kindred fathers '=' the ties of kinship between our fathers '.

Notice how in this phrase Latin prefers a concrete expression where we prefer an abstract one. Cf. **cum Caesar occisus aliis optimum, aliis pessimum facinus videretur,** ' since the killing of Caesar seemed to some a very good deed, to others a very wicked one.'

tua . . . fama, ' thy repute widespread upon earth '.

et fatis . . . volentem, lit. ' and by fate have led (me) willing ', i.e. ' by fate impelled me unresisting '. **fatis** is abl. of cause.

l. 135. **Electra,** abl. of origin, with **cretus. Atlantide** agrees with it. **ut,** ' as '.

l. 136. **advehitur,** historic present. The passive of **veho** is used as a deponent verb in the meaning ' sail ', as in l. 58.

Teucros, in prose **ad Teucros.** This acc. is called the acc. of the goal of motion.

l. 139. **Cyllenae . . . fudit,** ' conceived and brought forth on the cold summit of Cyllene '. The latter is a mountain in Arcadia. For the translation, cf. the note on l. 124, and the Latin for ' they captured and killed the messenger ', **nuntium captum interfecerunt.**

l. 140. **auditis . . . credimus,** ' if we believe the report at all ' =' if we have any belief in the report '. **auditis,** lit. ' (things) heard ', dat. dependent upon **credimus.**

ll. 140, 1. **at Maiam idem Atlas generat,** ' but of Maia this same Atlas is the sire '.

generat, ' is sire of ', an idiomatic use of the present : the action is past, but the present result is dwelt upon.

l. 142. **amborum,** supply **nostrum,** ' of both of us '. **scindit se,** ' divides itself ', i.e. ' divides ' or ' branches off '.

ll. 143, 4. **his fretus . . . pepigi,** ' in trust thereon, (I sent) not envoys, nor made my first soundings of thee by cunning '.

The above translation supplies a verb like **misi** (from **pepigi**) to govern **legatos**—an instance of zeugma.[1]

It is also possible to render : ' I decided upon no (sending of) envoys and no sounding of thee '.

per artem may also be rendered by an adj. ' subtle ' with **temptamenta.**

l. 145. **supplex,** ' (as) a suppliant '.

ll. 146, 7. **genus eadem . . . insequitur,** ' the same Rutulian race which (pursues) thee, pursues (us) with cruel war'.

Daunus, a legendary king of Apulia, was said to be the father or ancestor of Turnus. Hence ' Daunian ' =' Rutulian '; the Rutulians were the tribe over which Turnus ruled.

ll. 147–9. **nos . . . infra,** ' they believe that if they repel us, nothing will be lacking but that they send . . . and possess . . . ' (i.e. ' that nothing will prevent them from sending . . . and possessing . . .')

l. 149. **et mare . . .,** ' the sea which (washes Italy) above and

---

[1] A figure of speech in which a verb does duty with two nouns to one of which it is strictly applicable while the other appropriate verb is not used, cf. Shakespeare; ' kill the boys and (destroy) the luggage'.

which washes (Italy) below ', i.e. ' the Upper and Lower Seas ', the names which the Romans gave to the Tuscan and Adriatic seas respectively.

ll. 150, 1. **sunt nobis,** ' there are to us ' = ' we have '.

animi, ' courage '. **rebus . . . iuventus,** ' warriors proved in action '. The collective noun **iuventus** = **iuvenes,** for which see note on l. 105.

l. 152. **dixerat,** ' had spoken ', i.e.' ceased '. **ille,** Evander.

loquentis, ' of (him) speaking ', depends upon **os oculosque ;** translate ' his face and eyes as he spoke '.

l. 153. **iamdudum lustrabat,** ' had this long time been scanning '.

Latin uses present and imperfect where we have perfect and pluperfect for actions in the past which continue into the present, e.g. ' I have been waiting for you a long time ', **te iam diu exspecto.**

lumine = **oculo** as often in poetry.

l. 154. **ut,** ' how '. Translate with **libens,** adj. for adverb, ' how gladly '.

l. 155. **ut,** ' how ' again : to be taken with **recordor.**

ll. 157–9. **nam memini . . . fines.** Order for translation : **nam memini Priamum Laomedontiaden visentem** (when-he-came-to-visit) **regna sororis Hesionae** (et) **petentem** (and sought) **Salamina protinus invisere** (came-on-to-visit) **gelidos fines Arcadiae.**

Laomedontiaden, Greek acc. ending, 1st declension.

Salamina, Greek acc. ending, 3rd declension.

Hesione was a sister of Priam, king of Troy.

l. 160. **mihi.** Latin often uses the dat. of a personal pronoun where we prefer a possessive adj. In other words, translate **mihi** as though it were **meas** in agreement with **genas.**

vestibat, an older form of **vestiebat.**

iuventas, nom. sg. : **prima,** in agreement, ' early '.

l. 162. **cunctis,** abl. of comparison. **ibat,** ' moved '.

l. 163. **mihi.** See the note on l. 160. Translate here as if you had **mea** in agreement with **gens.**

l. 164. **dextrae, dextram,** here mean ' hand ' simply.

l. 165. **cupidus,** adj. for adv. ' eagerly '.

Pheneus in Arcadia seems to have been one of the fortresses of Evander.

ll. 166–8. **ille . . . Pallas.** Begin with **discedens,** ' departing ', i.e. ' on his departure '. **Lycias :** like his contemporary and friend Horace, Vergil frequently used proper names to secure increased vividness and concreteness and also to make full use of any euphony or melodiousness in their sound. The Lycians (from Asia Minor) were said to be famous for their skill as archers.

chlamydem auro intertextam. The Greeks and Romans were very fond of cloth embroidered with very fine gold thread. Note the spondee in the 5th foot.

frenaque . . . Pallas : order for translation : **-que bina** =duo) **aurea frena quae nunc meus Pallas habet.**
Pallas is the son of Evander.

l. 169. **ergo et . . . dextra,** ' therefore the hand that ye seek has been joined by me (=I have joined with thine) in treaty '.

mihi, dat. of the agent, a use found in verse with the passive voice.

foedere, abl. of respect.

l. 170. **et lux . . . cum primum,** ' as soon as '. **terris se reddet,** lit. ' shall give itself back to the earth ' =' shall revisit the earth '.

l. 172. **sacra haec annua,** ' this annual festival '. **quando,** ' since '. **amici,** ' (as) friends '.

l. 173. **quae nefas.** Supply **est. faventes,** ' graciously ', lit. ' favouring '.

l. 174. **iam nunc** =statim, ' at once '.

l. 175. **dicta,** supply **sunt.**

sublata, perf. part. pass. of tollo, ' having been removed ',

='which had been removed'. The cups had been removed when the Trojans first appeared.

l. 176. **ipse**, ' he himself', here ='in person '.

gramineo sedili, local abl. without preposition, ' on a . . . '

ll. 177, 8. **praecipuum accipit Aenean**, 'and with-special-honour he welcomes Aeneas.'

toro . . . leonis, lit. ' with a couch and the hide of a shaggy lion', instrumental abls. We would prefer to say ' to a couch . . . ' Similarly with **solio acerno**, lit. ' with a throne of maple ', i.e. ' to a maple throne '.

l. 179. **sacerdos**, nom. sg., subject with **lecti iuvenes** of **ferunt**. **certatim** is an adv., ' emulously ', with **ferunt**. Instead of ' emulously bring ', say ' vie with one another in bringing '.

l. 180. **onerant canistris dona**. We should expect **onerant canistra donis**, ' load the baskets with gifts ', but Vergil often avoids the obvious.

l. 181. **dona laboratae Cereris**, either ' gifts of Ceres (=bread) fashioned well ', or ' gifts of Ceres, won with toil '. In both translations the participle **laboratae** goes in sense with **dona**, in grammar with **Cereris**—a figure known as hypallage.

The names of gods and goddesses are often used in the poets for the things with which they are most closely associated. In this line **Bacchum** ='wine '.

l. 183. **perpetui tergo bovis**, ' the long chine of an ox '—hypallage again, for **perpetui** goes in grammar with **bovis**, but in sense with **tergo**. The latter is abl., as also is **lustralibus extis**, ' meat of purification ' ='sacrificial meat ', because **vescitur**, ' feeds on ', takes that case.

l. 184. **postquam . . . edendi**, a line imitated from Homer's, Now when they had got rid of their desire for food and drink '. Vergil however makes no reference to their thirst but mentions hunger twice—a repetition which is almost a characteristic of his style.

postquam ='when '. **exempta, compressus**. Supply **est** to give the perfect indic. pass.

ll. 185–8. **non haec . . . imposuit.** Retain the Latin order of three direct objects, one subject and verb, and put **non** with **vana superstitio,** translating by ' no ', and leave **nobis** to the last.

has ex more dapes, ' this in accordance with custom feast ', =' this accustomed feast '.

(non) vana . . . deorum, ' no superstition, idle and ignorant of the gods of old '.

ll. 188, 9. **saevis servati periclis,** ' (as men) rescued from cruel perils'.

facimus, ' we are sacrificing'. The verb is used here absolutely.

ll. 190 sqq. **iam primum . . .** Now follows the story of Cacus and Hercules, which is also told by Livy in Bk. I, 7. For purposes of comparison the text from Livy is included in this edition with a few notes, in Appendix A. It is interesting to note that according to the Roman historian the cult of Hercules was the only foreign worship introduced by Romulus. As the Greek hero was idealised by the Stoics for his endurance, simple living, and courage in the service of mankind, three qualities which in Vergil's day Romans felt had been the secret of their own greatness, it is natural that Vergil should emphasise that the Hercules cult is no idle superstition like so many rites introduced specially from the East and that he should thus indirectly support the religious policy of Augustus, who aimed at reviving the old Roman religion.

Evander opens his story by directing the attention of Aeneas to a nearby crag, around which shattered rocks point to some vast convulsion having occurred there.

l. 190. **saxis . . . rupem,** lit. ' behold this cliff overhung with rocks '=' this rocky overhanging cliff '.

l. 191. **disiectae . . . moles. ut,** ' how '. **moles,** ' boulders ' split off from the **rupes** of l. 190. **disiectae,** supply **sunt.**

ll. 191, 2. **desertaque . . . ruinam,** ' and (how) the mountain dwelling stands desolate, and the (fallen) rocks have spread wide ruin.'

stat, traxere. We may explain the indicative mood in the indirect question by taking the **ut** clause as exclamatory and therefore independent of the verb **aspice**.

l. 193. **hic**, adverb. **fuit**, ' was once '. The perfect implies ' and is no more '.

vasto . . . recessu, lit. ' moved on in an endless retirement ', =' stretching back endlessly '.

l. 194. **semihominis**. **semihomi**- is a dactyl, – ◡ ◡, the ' h ' being disregarded, and the ' i ' preceding it ranking as a semi-consonant, and being pronounced like the English ' *y* '.

l. 196. **adfixa**, ' nailed '; in agreement with **ora** in the next line.

l. 197. **virum**, gen. pl.

l. 198. **illius** =**Volcani**.

ll. 198, 9. **illius . . . ferebat**, lit. ' spouting his smoky flames from his mouth, he moved in mighty bulk '. To throw the emphasis on **illius** (emphatic in Latin by position), we must translate, ' his were the smoky flames that, as he moved in all his mighty bulk, he spouted from his mouth '.

l. 200. **et nobis**, ' even to us ', (as to others). **aetas**, ' time '.

l. 201. **maximus ultor**, ' the greatest of avengers ', is Hercules (Greek Heracles), the most popular and widely wor-shipped of heroes. He is called avenger because he delivered the human race from so many scourges.

l. 202. **superbus**, ' exulting ', to be taken with **nece spoliisque**.

tergemini Geryonae, ' of triple Geryon '. The tenth of the twelve labours of Hercules was to go to an island in the far west, Erytheia,[1] destroy the triple-bodied monster Geryon, and seize his cattle. This labour (with the remaining two, the stealing of Cerberus, watch-dog of Hell, and the plucking of the golden apples from the garden of the Hesperides in the West) is regarded as a more elaborate version of the ancient belief that Hercules met and overcame Hades.

l. 203. **Alcides**, lit. ' son of Alceus '. Actually Alceus was the

[1] lit. ' the blushing one ', i.e. ' sunset-coloured '.

grandfather of Hercules, for he was the father of Amphitryon.
See the note on l. 103.

victor, ' in his triumph '.

l. 204. **tenebant,** ' occupied ' or ' filled '. **boves** is the subject.

vallem amnemque. This is the low ground, stretching from
the Palatine Hill to the Tiber, which was later called the Forum
Boarium or cattle market. In it stood the Ara Maxima, the
most ancient place of worship of Hercules in Rome.

l. 205. **furis,** gen. of **fur.** There is another reading, **furiis,**
which if correct must be taken with **effera,** ' infuriated ',
' frenzied '.

ll. 205, 6. **ne quid . . . fuisset,** ' lest aught of crime or treachery should prove to have been undared or untried ', =' that no
crime or treachery might . . .'

sceleris, doli, partitive gen. dependent upon **quid.**

fuisset. Note this unusual tense in a purpose clause and the
way the translation tries to express its force.

l. 207. **praestanti corpore,** abl. of description or quality, ' of
outstanding strength '. **forma superante** in the next line is the
same construction.

l. 209. **ne qua . . . rectis,** lit. ' lest there should be any tracks
with the feet right ', i.e. ' pointing in the right direction '.

qua, from the indefinite adj. **qui, qua, quod,** ' any '. **forent** =
essent.

l. 210. **tractos, raptos** (l. 211). Read again the note on l. 124
and translate as if the text had **traxit et rapuit et. . . .**

ll. 210, 11. **versis . . . indiciis,** ' the signs of the passage having been reversed ', i.e. ' reversing the signs . . .'

l. 211. **saxo opaco,** ' within . . .' **occultabat,** ' was keeping
them hidden '.

l. 212. **quaerenti,** ' to one seeking ', =' to one who sought '.

ferebant, ' appeared to lead '.

l. 213. **stabulis,** ' from . . . ', abl. of separation.

l. 214. **Amphitryoniades.** See the note on l. 103.

ll. 215, 16. **discessu,** 'at parting'. **mugire,** historic infin., to be translated by a past tense of the indicative. **impleri** and **relinqui** are similar. Note carefully that the last two infins. are passive.

colles clamore relinqui, 'the hills were left (by the cattle) with lowing'. This verb might be better in the active in English, as also **impleri,** with **boves** as the subject. We should then have a common subject to the three verbs **mugire, impleri, relinqui.**

l. 217. **una boum,** i.e. one of the stolen heifers.

reddidit vocem, 'returned the sound', i.e. 'lowed in answer'.

sub, 'in-the-depths-of'.

l. 218. **custodita,** '(though) guarded closely'. Latin participles often have a concessive meaning.

l. 219. **hic,** adv., 'at this'. **Alcidae . . . dolor,** 'the wrath of Hercules blazed forth furiously (**furiis**) with black gall'. The pluperfect **exarserat** expresses the instantaneous reaction of Hercules.

l. 220. **nodis . . . robur,** lit. 'his oak heavy with knots', ='his heavy club of gnarled oak'. This club was the traditional weapon of Hercules.

l. 221. **ardua,** neut. pl. acc., 'the heights'. The 'towering hill' is the Aventine which rises to a height of about 100 feet.

l. 222. **nostri,** in agreement with **oculi,** nom. pl. **videre,** perfect indic. as the scansion. vĭdērĕ shows : the pres. infin. act. is vĭdērĕ.

l. 223. **euro,** abl. of comparison.

l. 225. **ut,** 'when'.

ruptis . . . saxum. The entrance to the cave seems to have been defended by a primitive portcullis which consisted of a boulder hung upon chains. In his panic, 'Cacus broke the chains and let fall the huge rock'.

Note once again that the Latin participle **ruptis** is rendered in English by a finite verb.

l. 226. **ferro et arte paterna,** lit. ' by his father's iron and cunning ', i.e. ' by his father's skill in iron-work '.

The father of Cacus is Vulcan.

quod, ' which '.

l. 227. **fultos . . . postes,** lit. ' and with its barrier blocked the secured entrance ', =' secured and blocked the entrance '.

See again the end of the note to l. 225.

postes, lit. ' door-posts ', is used for the ' doorway ', ' entrance '. This figure of speech is known as synecdoche, or ' part for the whole '. It is found in English poetry as well as in Latin.

l. 228. **Tirynthius,** another name for Hercules. Tiryns, **a** town in South Greece, was the place where Hercules was brought up.

l. 229. **ora ferebat,** ' turned his gaze '.

l. 232. **limina,** pl. for sg., and another example of synecdoche, for **limen,** properly ' threshold ', is used for ' door '.

valle, local abl. ' in . . .'

l. 233. **acuta silex,** ' a tapering (pillar of) flint '. **praecisis . . . saxis,** ' the rock cut sheer away on all sides ', i.e. the crag stood alone.

l. 234. **speluncae . . . visu,** ' rising up from the back of the cave, most high to view ', lit. ' in the seeing '. **visu,** abl. of respect.

l. 235. **domus,** ' a place '. **dirarum volucrum,** ' of fearful birds ', probably birds of prey, vultures, kites or the like.

ll. 236–9. **hanc . . . impulit,** ' this (pillar) as it leaned forward **(prona)** from the ridge towards the river on-the-left, he shook and loosened **(concussit et solvit),** pressing full against it from-the-right **(nitens in adversum dexter)** and tearing it from its lowest foundations **(avulsam imis radicibus)** ', lit. ' torn from its lowest roots '. **avulsam,** perf. part. pass. in agreement with **hanc.**

The rock jutted over the river on the left ; Hercules, thrusting against it from the right, pushed it into the river.

l. 241. **detecta apparuit**, 'was seen (to be) unroofed'.

l. 243. **non secus ac si**, 'not otherwise than if' = ' just as if '.

qua . . . dehiscens reseret, 'the earth, gaping wide beneath some force (**qua vi**), were to reveal '.
Note the mood and tense, present subj. of **reseret**, and the translation. The following verbs, **recludat, cernatur, trepident**, are similar, and should be translated similarly.

l. 245. **super** = desuper, ' from above '.

l. 246. **manes**. Note this word, 3rd decl. masc. with the **a** long, and distinguish it carefully from **mănus**, 4th decl. fem., with **a** short.

immisso lumine, abl. absol., ' the light having been let in ', = ' as the light flooded in '.

l. 247. **deprensum**, in agreement with **eum** understood (= Cacum), as are also **inclusum, rudentem** in the next line.
It will be a help to retain the order of the Latin, provided it is remembered that the words mentioned above are in the acc., object of **premit**, the verb, **Alcides** being the subject.

l. 248. **insueta rudentem**, 'uttering strange roars'. **insueta**, acc. pl. neut., adverbial accusative (sometimes called an internal acc.).

l. 250. **vastis molaribus**. The boulders which Hercules rained upon Cacus were as large as mill-stones.

l. 251. **ille**, i.e. Cacus. **super** = superest, ' is left '. **pericli** depends upon **fuga**, ' from danger '. For the gen., see the note on l. 46.

l. 252. **ingentem fumum**, ' a great (cloud of) smoke '.

mirabile dictu, lit. ' wonderful in the telling ', i.e. ' to relate '.

l. 254. **prospectum . . . oculis**, ' stealing (lit. taking away) all view from the eyes '. **oculis** is a dat. of disadvantage, which is commonly found with compound verbs meaning ' to take away '.

sub antro, ' in the cave beneath '. Cf. l. 217.

l. 256. **non tulit**, ' (could) not endure (this) '. **animis**, ' in his fury ' an abl. of cause. **ipse** can be ignored in translation.

ll. 257, 8. **qua . . . agit,** lit. ' where most smoke drives the billow ' = ' where the smoke swirls most densely '.

l. 258. **nebula,** abl. as the scansion shows. **atra** is in agreement with it : ' the huge cave eddies with the black pall.' In English we should prefer ' the pall ' as subject : ' the black pall eddies in the huge cave '.

l. 259. **hic,** adv.

l. 260. **in nodum complexus,** lit. ' having embraced (him) into a knot ', i.e. ' in knot-like embrace '.

ll. 260, 1. **et angit . . . guttur,** lit. ' and, clinging close, he strangles his starting eyes and throat drained of blood '.

angit, ' chokes ', ' throttles ', goes more properly with **guttur** than with **oculos. elisos,** lit. ' squeezed out '.

As **elisos** and **siccum** seem to be proleptic, we might render : ' throttles him until his eyes start from his head and his throat is drained of blood '.

l. 262. **foribus revulsis.** Translate this abl. absol. first as a main verb, ' the doors are torn off ', i.e. by Hercules from the inside.

l. 263. **abiuratae,** ' denied on oath '. The poet suggests that Cacus had sworn that he had not stolen the cattle.

l. 265. **nequeunt . . . corda** is nom., ' our hearts '; ' our ' because Evander is relating to Aeneas and his followers the story of events in which he took part himself.

l. 268. **ex illo** : supply **tempore,** ' from that time '. **celebratus,** supply **est. minores,** supply **natu,** ' (those) less by birth ' = ' the younger ones ', ' posterity '.

l. 269. **primus . . . :** supply **erat.**
For the connection of the two families, the Potitii and the Pinarii, with the worship of Hercules, see also the extract from Livy, Bk. I, 7, in the Appendix.

l. 271. **statuit.** Hercules is the subject. **hanc aram** is the Ara Maxima in the Forum Boarium, to which reference has already been made in the note on l. 204.

l. 272. **et erit . . . semper.** Order for translation : **et quae semper erit maxima.**

l. 273. **agite,** ' come '. See the note on l. 59.

tantarum . . . laudum, ' in honour of such glorious deeds '.

laus, ' praise ', often means ' praiseworthy (=glorious) deed '.

l. 275. **communem deum,** ' our common god ' =' the god common to us both ' or ' whom we both worship '. ' We ' =' Arcadians and Trojans '.

volentes =' with good will '.

l. 276. **dixerat.** Turn back to the note on l. 152.

cum, ' when '. See again the note on l. 98.

pōpŭlŭs. The scansion (its position in the 5th foot shows that it is a dactyl) helps us to see that this word means ' poplar ', not the ' people ' (**pŏpŭlŭs**).

bicolor. The poplar is described as ' two-coloured ' because the leaves are whitish underneath. The tree was sacred to Hercules.

l. 277. **velavitque.** The **-que** means ' both ', and can be ignored in translation.

foliis innexa, ' fastened (to his hair) with its leaves '. (It may, however, be a variation for **foliis innexis,** ' its leaves plaited together '.) Evander had made a chaplet of poplar leaves to wear on his head.

l. 279. **laeti,** adj. for adv.

l. 280. **devexo Olympo,** ' as the heavens sink '. Note : (i) **devehor,** ' I am carried down ' is used practically as a deponent, ' I go down ', and may, therefore, use its perfect participle in a present meaning. (ii) The ancients believed the earth to be a circular plane around which the heavens revolved. Thus the sky is described as sinking below the western horizon as the evening approaches from the east.

Cf. Aeneid, II, 250, **vertitur interea caelum et ruit oceano nox.**

l. 282. **in morem,** ' after their fashion '. **flammas,** ' torches'.

l. 283. **mensae secundae,** gen. dependent upon **grata dona.**

l. 285. **Salii.** According to Livy, I. 20, the Roman king Numa appointed twelve Salii for the worship of Mars. The word is connected with **salio,** ' I leap ', and the priests were so named from their practice of honouring the god with ritual dances. Hercules seems to have had his ' dancers ' too.

ad cantus, ' for songs ' =' to sing '.

l. 286. **evincti tempora,** ' having bound their temples '. **tempora** is the object of **evincti** which has an active meaning. In Greek there exists a third voice of the verb, called the middle, which, as its name suggests, partakes of the nature of both active and passive, since it has very largely the same *forms* as the latter, but the *meaning* of the former, together with the notion that the act is done reflexively, *to* or *for* the doer. The Roman poets, who were very much influenced by the content and the technique of the Greek poets whom they consciously imitated, introduced this construction into their verse, and for the reasons given above, it is said to be an instance of ' the middle use of the passive voice '.

l. 287. **iuvenum,** ' of youths ' here, not as in l. 105, etc. **laudes,** see the note on l. 273.

l. 288. **ferunt :** see the Vocabulary.

ut, ' how ', introducing an indirect question.

prima, in grammar an adj. with **monstra,** is to be taken adverbially with **eliserit:** ' first '.

novercae. His step-mother is Juno, if his real father was Jupiter. In her jealousy she sent two serpents to destroy Hercules when he was a mere baby.

l. 289. **monstra . . . angues.** Ignore the -que in translation and take **monstra** in apposition with **geminos angues.**

l. 290. **ut idem,** ' how the same man ' =' how he also '.

l. 291. **Troiam . . .** In both cities, Hercules had been cheated by the king and his action was taken for revenge.

mille. Twelve is the usual number of the labours of Hercules.

l. 292. **rege sub Eurystheo.** Eurystheus was king of Mycenae and related to Hercules. It was at the bidding of Juno that he imposed the famous twelve labours on the hero. Juno's enmity pursued him relentlessly all his life.

ll. 293–5. **tu . . . leonem.** We are now at part of the hymn of the Salii in direct speech, which continues as far as line 302. **mactas,** ' thou killest ', =' art the slayer of ', has three objects, ' the cloud-born (centaurs) of double shape, H. and P. ', ' the Cretan monsters ' and ' the huge lion beneath the rock of Nemea '. ' The Cretan monsters ' (plur. for sg.) is a reference to the wild boar which plagued Erymanthus in Crete. The slaying of this creature and of the Nemean lion are two of the labours Hercules had to perform.

Centaurs are wild creatures, half man and half horse, who according to one legend were begotten by Ixion when he attempted to ravish Juno[1] the wife of Jupiter.[1] The goddess, however, was replaced by a cloud-image of her, and from this union with the cloud were sprung the centaurs.

ll. 296, 7. **te . . . cruento. te,** ' at thee ' ; it is the object of **tremuere,** ' trembled (at) '. **super** is a prep. governing **semesa ossa.** With **ianitor Orci** supply **tremuit.**

Another of Hercules' labours was to go down to the under-world and carry off the triple-headed watch-dog, Cerberus.

ll. 298, 9. **nec . . . tenens,** ' no (other) shape (could) terrify thee, nay, not even (**ipse**) Typhoeus, towering with weapons in his hands '.

Typhoeus, a giant, destroyed by Jupiter and buried under Mt. Aetna, is mentioned here as a typical monster.

ll. 299, 300. **non . . . anguis,** lit. ' thee not lacking counsel, the Lernaean Hydra surrounded with its throng of heads '. ' thou wast not lacking . . . when the L. H. . . .' The Hydra was a monster of many heads, which lived near a stream and marsh called Lerna not far from Argos. Its destruction and the draining of the marsh was one of Hercules' labours.

l. 301. **vera proles,** ' true child of J.'. His glorious deeds reveal his true father, Jupiter.

[1] The Greek names Hera, Zeus, would be more appropriate.

addite, voc. sing. masc., is in agreement with **tu** understood. **decus** is to be taken with it ; ' an added glory '.

l. 302. **dexter,** adj. for adv. ' graciously '. **adi,** imperative of the verb **adeo.**

l. 304. **speluncam Caci,** ' the (tale of) Cacus' cavern '.

l. 307. **referunt. referre** used reflexively often means ' return ', lit. ' to bear oneself back '.

ll. 308, 9. **et comitem . . . ingrediens,** ' and as-he-moved (**ingrediens**) he kept Aeneas and his son close-by-him (**iuxta**) (as) companions '.

l. 310. **faciles,** ' easily moving ', i.e. ' restless '.

l. 311. **et.** The conjunction links **capitur,** ' is charmed ', with **exquirit** in the next line. **-que** after the latter verb means ' both ' and can be ignored.

laetus, adj. for adv., ' joyfully '.

l. 314. **haec nemora,** acc. **indigenae** is an adj. of the 1st decl. only, here in agreement with **Fauni Nymphaeque. tenebant,** ' inhabited '.

l. 315. **truncis et duro robore,** abl. of origin with **nata,** ' sprung from . . .'

l. 316. **quīs** =quibus, ' to whom there was . . .' = ' who had neither (*neque*) . . .'

l. 317. **norant** =noverant, ' knew *how* to '.

parcere parto, lit. ' to spare that-having-been-won ', i.e. ' to husband what they had won '. Note : (i) **parco** is followed by the dative. (ii) **parto** is from the verb, **pario, -ere, peperi, partum,** ' I beget ', ' produce '; ' win ', ' acquire '.

l. 318. **asper victu venatus,** lit. ' hunting rough in-the-fare (it gives) '. We might turn this by : ' the huntsman's rough fare '.

l. 319. **Saturnus.** Although it is tempting to explain Saturn as ' a god of the sowing ' and regard his name as connected with **sero,** ' I sow ', many difficulties incline us to follow the ancients themselves, who regarded him as an importation from Greece and thus identified him with Kronos, who was eventually dethroned and expelled from Greece by his son Zeus. In this role Saturnus was regarded as one who brought the benefits of civilisation to Italy and introduced ' a golden age '.

l. 320. **regnis . . . ademptis**, ' an exile from the kingdom that had been taken (from him) '.

l. 321. **is**, ' he ', i.e. Saturn.

l. 322. **Latiumque . . .** The derivation of **Latium** from **lateo** is fanciful and appears to be Vergil's own. Supply **terram** before **Latium**.

l. 323. **latuisset**. The subjunctive is used because Vergil is giving us not *his* reason, but the reason in Saturn's mind. The causal **quoniam** clause is therefore *virtually* subordinate in indirect speech.

ll. 324, 5. **aurea . . . saecula**. Order for translation : **sub illo rege fuere saecula quae perhibent aurea**.

l. 326. **deterior ac decolor aetas**, ' a baser and less lustrous age'. The phrase maintains the metaphor which was begun by the phrase ' golden age '. Its successor is ' the silver age '.

l. 327. **amor habendi**, ' the love of having ' =' the desire for gain '.

l. 328. **vēnēre = venerunt**.

l. 329. **saepius**, as often in verse, =**saepe**.

posuit, ' laid aside '.

l. 330. **asperque . . . Thybris**, ' and fierce Thybris of the mighty frame '. We seem to have a reference here to legends in which Thybris was originally a local chieftain.

l. 331. **Itali**, ' we Italians ', or better, ' we of Italy ' **Itali** is nom. pl. in apposition with the unexpressed subject of **diximus**.

ll. 333–6. **me . . . Apollo**. Retain the Latin order by translating the object **me** first and then the participles which are in agreement with **me**.

Evander was driven from Arcadia, his native home (**patriā**) either by the Argives, his enemies, or by famine. To a Greek sailing westwards, it might seem that he was ' seeking the ends of the sea '.

Carmentis Nymphae. Most of the heroes of epic have divine or semi-divine blood in their veins. Carmentis (the mother of Evander) was a prophetic goddess.

deus auctor Apollo, lit. ' the god Apollo, suggester ' = 'Apollo's divine suggestion.' Repeat **me** as the object of **egere**(=**egerunt**).

l. 337. **dicta.** Supply **sunt. dehinc,** lit. ' hence ', is here best translated ' (when) . . . from there '.

et =' both ', but it can be ignored.

l. 338. **Romani nomine** belongs to **quam memorant** in the next line, ' which the Romans call by the name Carmental '.

l. 339. **Nymphae . . . honorem,** ' an ancient tribute to the nymph Carmentis '. For the gen. **Nymphae,** see the note on l. 46. The phrase is in apposition to the previous clause **quam . . . memorant.**

l. 340. **cecinit,** .' prophesied '.

ll. 340, 1. **cecinit . . . Pallanteum.** Order for translation : **quae prima cecinit Aeneadas futuros (esse) magnos et Pallanteum (futurum) nobile.**

l. 342. **hinc,** lit. ' hence ', =' next ' here.

ll. 342–4. Order for translation : **hinc monstrat ingentem lucum quem acer Romulus rettulit asylum, et sub gelida rupe Lupercal dictum de Parrhasio more Panos Lycaei.**

rettulit, ' made ' or ' created '. The asylum or ' sanctuary ' on the Capitol was intended by Romulus to house the refugees whom he wished to attract in order to increase the population of his new city.

Lupercal. The Lupercal was a cavern under the west corner of the Palatine Hill. It was connected as a shrine with the worship of Faunus, an Italian pastoral and woodland deity, who was later identified with the Greek god Pan, a god of herdsmen and native to Arcadia.

Vergil assumes that the dedication of the Lupercal to Pan Lycaeus was made by Evander and his Arcadians.

The epithet **Lycaeus** is used of Pan because it seemed to be derived from the Greek word for ' wolf ', and thus reminded the Romans of Lupercal, connected in its turn, with **lupus,** ' a wolf '. It would be natural for a pastoral community such as early Rome was, to have worshipped or propitiated a wolf-god, if only to keep off the wolves from their herds. Finally, to the Romans this cave or grotto would be linked with their most famous national legend, the suckling of Romulus and Remus by a she-wolf.

l. 344. **Parrhasio** means ' Arcadian ', from the town Parrhasia in Arcadia.

Panos Lycaei. Panos is a Greek gen. sg. form. With this genitive, we have to supply some such word as ' place ' or ' shrine '.

l. 345. **nec non et,** ' nor-not also ' =' and moreover, '. The two negatives cancel out.

l. 345. **Argiletum.** Vergil derives the name of this district in Rome behind the north-east part of the Forum, which was in later times the centre of handicraftsmen and booksellers, from **Argi-letum,** ' the death of Argus '. The name is more plausibly derived from **argilla,** ' potter's clay ', which was found in the district.

It is uncertain who this Argus, guest of Evander, was. In mythology there is an Argus, a monster of huge size and strength who had many eyes. He is said, however, to have been slain by the god Hermes (Mercury).

l. 346. **testaturque locum,** ' and he calls the place to witness ', i.e. that his guest was killed deservedly.

l. 347. **ad Tarpeiam sedem,** ' to the Tarpeian dwelling '. Vergil's Roman readers would immediately think of the most famous of all Roman temples, the Capitol, which had been dedicated in the first year of the Republic, 509 B.C., to a group of three deities, Jupiter Optimus Maximus, Minerva, and Juno. Another association would also arise from the name ' Tarpeian ', for the Tarpeian rock at the south-west corner of the Capitoline

Hill was the place from which murderers and traitors were thrown.

l. 348. **aurea nunc,** ' golden now ', i.e. in Vergil's day. The temple was said to have had a gilded roof.

l. 349. **iam tum,** ' even then '. **religio dira loci,** ' the dread sanctity of the place '. **terrebat,** ' awed '.

ll. 351, 2. **hoc . . . deus.** Retain the order of the Latin and render **habitat deus,** lit. ' a god dwells in ', by ' is the dwelling-place of a god '.

l. 354. **aegida,** Greek acc. sg. The aegis is represented by a goatskin and regarded as an attribute of Zeus (Jupiter) and Athena (Minerva). In its association with the latter in art it was bordered with snakes and bore the head of Medusa in the centre. In epic convention the aegis inspired enemies with terror and gave confidence to friends.

dextra. Scan the line to determine the length of the final syllable and hence its case, short a nom., long a abl.

ll. 355, 6. **haec duo . . . virorum.** Translate l. 355 first, then in order insert ' which ' before **vides** and ' are ' before **reliquias . . . virorum.**

l. 357. **Ianus.** According to the myth, Janus was an ancient king of Latium, who hospitably received Saturn when he was expelled by his son from Crete. Later he seems to have become a god of beginnings—a development which arose from his being a god of gates. In art he was represented with two faces directed in opposite ways. Vergil calls him **Ianus bifrons** in XII, 198.

l. 358. **Ianiculum.** The Janiculum is a prominent ridge on the west bank of the Tiber at Rome about three and a half miles long. It faces the Capitol.

Saturnia is an old name for the Capitol.

l. 361. **lautis Carinis,** like **Romano foro,** is a local abl. without the preposition **in.** The Carinae was in Vergil's day a fashionable quarter of Rome on the Esquiline Hill.

l. 362. **ut,** ' when '. **ventum** (est to be supplied). Intransitive verbs are frequently used impersonally in the passive in Latin. They are often rendered into English *personally* and in the *active* : e.g. **pugnatum est** ='they fought'. **limina,** pl. for sg.

l. 363. **subiit.** The final syllable is lengthened by its position in the foot. Cf. the note on **procul,** l. 98.

l. 364. **dignum deo,** 'worthy of divinity', i.e. to be like Hercules, who after death was placed among the gods.

l. 365. **rebusque . . . egenis.** The scansion **vĕnī** shows that this form of the verb is the 2nd sg. pres. imper. act.: 'and come not disdainful of (lit. harsh to) our needy state'.

l. 366. **dixit . . .** 'he spake and beneath the roof. . . .'

l. 367. **Aenean,** Greek acc. sg. ending. **stratis,** local abl. again.

l. 368. **stratisque . . . effultum,** 'made-him-to recline upon a couch, supported, by (i.e. resting on). . . .'

l. 369. **nox ruit,** 'night rushes down'.

l. 370. **haud . . . mater,** lit. 'a mother not vainly terrified in her heart' ='her mother's heart dismayed by no vain terrors'.

l. 371. **Laurentum,** gen. pl., dependent upon **minis.**

l. 372. **Volcanum.** In mythology Vulcan (in Greek Hephaestus) is the husband of Venus (Aphrodite) and armourer of the gods.

haec, 'thus', lit. 'these things' with **incipit** in the next line.

ll. 374, 5. **Pergama debita . . . arces.** 'Pergama owed (to destruction) =doomed, and her towers destined-to-fall (**casuras**) amid hostile flames'.

Pergama, strictly the name of the citadel of Troy and neuter plural, is often used for Troy itself.

l. 377. **artis opisque tuae,** 'of thy skill and power.' **te** is the object, as is **tuos labores** in the next line, of **exercere,** 'to task'.

l. 378. **-ve,** lit. 'or', must be rendered into English by 'nor'. It links **te** and **labores.**

l. 379. **deberem plurima**, lit. ' I owed very much ' = ' my debt was very great '.

l. 381. **oris**, ' on the . . .' ; another local abl.

ll. 382, 3. **ergo eadem . . . nato.** There are three interesting points in this sentence : (i) **eadem** = ' after all '. The full meaning in **eadem**, ' I that *same* Venus who never asked anything before, am doing so now ', is sometimes rendered, ' who never asked before '. (ii) **sanctum numen, arma,** are two accusatives after **rogo,** a construction found in Latin after verbs of *asking, teaching,* and *concealing.* English says, ' I ask arms *of* the deity sacred to me '. (iii) **genetrix nato** is a good example of effective juxtaposition, ' a mother for her son '.

ll. 383, 4. **filia Nerei, Tithonia coniunx.** The daughter of Nereus (Thetis) and the wife of Tithonus (Aurora) made similar requests of Vulcan, viz. to make armour for their sons Achilles and Memnon respectively.

l. 385. **qui populi,** ' what peoples '. **quae moenia,** ' what walled cities '.

l. 386. **in** with **me** means ' against me ' ; with **excidium,** ' for the destruction of . . .', i.e. ' to destroy my people '.

l. 387. **dixerat.** See the note on l. 152.

hinc atque hinc, lit. ' from this side and from that ', should be taken closely with **niveis lacertis** and thus translated, ' throwing her snow-white arms around him '.

l. 388. **cunctantem,** ' (him) hesitating ', ' as he hesitated '.

l. 389. **notus,** lit. ' known ', = ' familiar '.

l. 391. **non secus atque cum,** ' not otherwise than when ' = ' even as when '. **olim,** ' at times '.

ll. 391, 2. **tonitru rupta . . . nimbos,** ' the fiery streak, bursting (**rupta**) with the thunder, runs flashing with dazzling light (**corusco lumine**) through the storm-clouds '.

l. 393. **sensit,** ' perceived (it) ', i.e. that she had caught him.

dolis, abl. of cause, ' in her wiles ', with **laeta.**

l. 394. **pater,** Vulcan.

l. 395. **ex alto**, ' from on-high ' = ' from so far away '. We, too, talk about ' far-fetched excuses '. Vulcan is referring to cases mentioned by Venus in ll. 383–4.

ll. 395, 6. **fiducia . . . mei?** ' whither, o goddess, has gone thy confidence in me? ' **mei** is obj. gen., i.e. the relation between it and the noun on which it depends, **fiducia**, is similar to that between an object and its governing verb.

ll. 396, 7. **similis si . . . fuisset, . . . fuisset.** Note the pluperfect subj., the tense and mood which are used in conditional clauses, unreal in past time. ' If like care had been thine, it would have been right . . .'

l. 398. **pater omnipotens**, ' the almighty father ', i.e. Jupiter.

l. 401. **quidquid curae**, ' whatever (of) care '. Note the partitive gen., frequent in Latin after nouns or neuter pronouns denoting amount.

l. 402. **quod**, ' whatever '. **liquido electro**, ' with molten electrum '. The latter is a metal, an alloy of gold and silver.

l. 403. **quantum . . . valent**, ' as much as fire and air avail ' = ' all the power of fire and air '.

After these subordinate clauses, we should expect Vergil to continue with a clause, ' all shall be thine '. Instead, he leaves his sentence unfinished and continues with an unconnected imperative.

ll. 405, 6. **placidumque . . . soporem**, ' and sinking on the bosom of his spouse, he sought peaceful slumber throughout his frame '. For the translation of **infusus**, read the note on l. 25, and note that English prefers the present tense for its participle, not the perfect as in the Latin.

l. 407. **medio . . . curriculo**, ' in the mid-career of departing night '. **abactae**, lit. ' driven away ' = ' banished ' = ' fleeting ' or ' departing '.

The first sleep, the soundest we are told, had now left Vulcan.

l. 408. **cum**, ' at the time when '.

ll. 409, 10. **cui . . . impositum (est)**, ' on whom it has been laid (i.e. whose heavy task it is) to support her life with her distaff and fine weaving '.

Minerva is the patron goddess of spinning and weaving, and her name is used here for weaving itself.

l. 411. **operi**, ' to her (day's) work '.

l. 411. **ad lumina longo penso**, ' by lamplight (lit. by the lights) at the long task '. **penso** is abl. of means.

l. 412. **castum**, proleptic : see the note on l. 37.

l. 414. **haud secus**, lit. ' not otherwise ', i.e. ' just so '. After this lovely domestic simile, Vergil now completes the picture with that of the god Vulcan rising to go to his work.

nec . . . illo, ' nor more slothful (than she) at that time ' =' and as active as she . . .'

ll. 416, 7. **insula . . . saxis**. Order for translation : **iuxta Sicanium latus -que Aeoliam Liparen erigitur** ' (there rises) ' **insula, ardua fumantibus saxis**.

The island is Hiera (mod. Volcano), one of the Lipari islands, as also is ' Aeolian Lipare '. They are volcanic.

For the translation of **erigitur**, see the note on l. 25.

l. 418. **quam subter** =**subter quam**—an example of what is called anastrophe. After these words translate next **tonant** and then the subjects **specus, antra Aetnaea**.

exesa caminis, ' hollowed out for the forges '.

ll. 419–20. **validique . . . gemitus**, ' and powerful blows are heard echoing sounds from the anvils '.

l. 421. **stricturae Chalybum**, ' (iron) bars of the Chalybes '. The latter were a people of Asia who were said to have been the first to forge iron. The use of the proper name adds picturesqueness, and is not to be understood too literally.

strictura lit. means ' a pressing ', and so the metal smelted from the ore.

l. 423. **hoc** =**huc**, ' hither '.

l. 425. **Brontes . . . Pyracmon**. The Cyclops were in mythology a one-eyed race of giants who lived on the coast of Sicily. They are the craftsmen of Vulcan who make thunderbolts for Jupiter. In Homer, however, they are a pastoral folk who lived in caves and spent their time tending their flocks and herds. The most famous was Polyphemus whom Odysseus (Ulysses) outwitted.

nudus membra, ' bare as to the limbs ' = ' bare-limbed '. **membra** is acc. of respect.

ll. 426, 7. **his informatum . . . erat,** lit. ' by them (dat. of the agent) a thunderbolt had been shaped in their hands, part being already polished ', i.e. ' with their hands they had shaped a thunderbolt and part polished it already '.

l. 427. **quae plurima,** ' (like those) which in large numbers '; **plurima,** lit. ' very many '.

l. 428. **pars . . .** Insert ' but ' or ' while ' before **pars.**

l. 429. **imbris torti,** ' of driving rain '.

radios, ' rays ' or ' shafts '. To understand this picture, we must remember that the conventional representation of a thunderbolt showed a hand grasping a bundle of darts. Vergil is here describing the various parts of a thunderstorm, cloud, rain, lighning and wind.

l. 432. **flammisque . . . iras,** ' and wrath with pursuing flames '.

l. 433. **parte alia,** ' in another part ', i.e. of the workshop.

l. 434 **.nstabant,** ' they were pressing upon ' = ' they were hard at work at '. It is unusual for the verb **instare** to be used transitively with direct objects as here.

l. 435. **aegida,** Greek 3rd decl. acc. sg. See again the note on l. 354. The phrase **in pectore** in l. 437 seems to suggest that Vergil is thinking of the representation of Pallas in which she wears the aegis as a cloak over her shoulders and covering her breast almost like a breastplate. Pallas also appears in art with the aegis worn like a shield over her left arm. Cf. the phrase in l. 354.

turbatae . . . arma, ' the armour of Pallas (when) roused '. Translate this line before rendering **certatim polibant** (=**polie-**

bant), lit. ' emulously they were polishing ' = ' they vied with each other in polishing '.

squamis . . . auroque, lit. ' with scales of serpents and with gold ' = ' with the golden scales of serpents ' ; an excellent example of an hendiadys, for an explanation of which see the note on l. 40.

ll. 437, 8. **conexosque . . . collo,** ' and the wreathed snakes and the Gorgon herself on the goddess' breast, turning her eyes, her neck severed '. For the last part we might say, ' and the severed head of the Gorgon herself on the goddess' breast, darting her glance '.

The head of Medusa, the Gorgon, had been severed by the hero Perseus. She had the power of turning to stone any person on whom she turned her gaze.

l. 439. **coeptos labores,** ' the tasks you have begun '.

l. 441. **arma . . . viro,** lit., ' arms (are) to-be-made for a brave hero (by you) '. The gerundive is passive in Latin : we, however, prefer the active voice and would say : ' you must make . . .' **vobis** has to be supplied with **facienda.**

ll. 441, 2. **nunc . . . usus,** ' there is need (to you) of strength . . .' i.e. ' now you need your strength . . .'.

Note the construction of **usus est.** Like **opus est,** it has ablative of the thing needed, dat. of the person who needs.

l. 443. **effatus.** Supply **est.**

l. 445. **sortiti.** Supply **sunt.**

fluit . . . metallum. fluit, though sing., has two subjects : **aes** and **auri metallum.** The latter means literally ' ore of gold ', = ' golden ore '. **rivis,** ' in streams ', abl. of manner.

ll. 447–9. **ingentem . . . impediunt,** ' a giant shield they shape, one against (=to face alone) all the weapons of the Latins, and bind seven plates on plates (=weld one plate upon another sevenfold) '.

orbes are the circular layers of metal.

l. 450. **stridentia aera,** plural for sing.

ll. 452, 3. **illi . . . massam,** ' with mighty force they raise their arms in rhythmic alternation and turn the metal with gripping tongs '.

inter sese in numerum, lit. ' among themselves in rhythm '.

l. 452 is an excellent example of the figure known as onomatopoeia, or the attempt to match sound with sense. Here the succession of four heavy spondees gives the impression of heavy blows falling alternately.

l. 454. **pater Lemnius.** ' The lord of Lemnos ' is Vulcan (Greek Hephaestus). The cult of the Greek god spread from Asia Minor westwards via the important island of Lemnos in the Aegean. According to mythology, Hephaestus on being ejected from Olympus by Zeus fell on the island, a fact which made it sacred to him.

l. 455. **suscitat.** The sing. verb has two subjects, **lux alma** and **matutini . . . cantus.** The order of the Latin can effectively be retained by turning the sentence into the passive, ' Evander is roused from his lowly home by the . . .'

l. 457. **tunicaque . . . artus. inducitur,** ' clothes ', is another example of the middle use of the passive voice. See the note on l. 286.

l. 458. **Tyrrhena,** ' Tuscan ', has no special significance here : it merely gives an antique flavour to the line. **plantis,** dat., but we say, ' puts . . . on the soles '.

l. 459. **Tegaeum** means ' Arcadian ', because Tegea is an important town in Arcadia. Vergil uses the name merely to give local colour.

l. 460. **demissa . . . retorquens,** ' flinging back the panther's hide that hung from the left '. Evander wished to have the hide out of the way of his sword, which he wore on his left side.

l. 461. **gemini custodes canes,** ' two watch-dogs '.

l. 463. **hospitis . . . petebat.** Retain some of the order of the Latin by translating: **sedem** ('lodging') **et secreta hospitis Aeneae heros petebat.** Evander's lowly home seems to have had no accommodation for visitors, for Aeneas is obviously staying away from the house of his host.

D2

l. 464. **promissi muneris,** ' of the help he had promised '.

l. 465. **nec minus . . . agebat,** ' and no less early Aeneas was moving himself (=was astir) '.

l. 466. **huic . . . illi,** dat. dependent upon **comes ibat,** ' went (as) companion to ' =' accompanied '. Strictly speaking, the pronouns in the order **hic . . . ille** mean ' the latter ', ' the former '. Render here, however, by ' the one ,' ' the other '.

l. 467. **mediis aedibus,** ' in the central court ', i.e. in the peristylium.

l. 469. **rex prior haec.** Supply **dixit.**

l. 470. **quo sospite,** abl. absol., ' who (being) safe '. Cf. **te consule,** ' you (being) consul ', i.e. ' in your consulship '. Similarly **quo sospite** =' in whose lifetime ' or ' while you live '.

l. 471. **res Troiae,** ' the might of Troy '. **victas (esse)** goes both with **res** and **regna.**

ll. 472, 3. **nobis . . . vires,** lit. ' to us for help of war in proportion to (our) so great name, scant (is) the strength ' ; i.e. ' we have but scant strength considering our great name, to aid thee in war '.

Evander is referring to the fact that it was his name and reputation that had attracted Aeneas in the hope of making an alliance.

l. 473. **Tusco amni.** The ' Tuscan stream ' is the Tiber. For much of its course, the Tiber was the boundary between Etruria and her neighbours in the north-east, east and south.

l. 475. **opulentaque regnis castra,** ' and a camp rich in kingdoms '. The phrase refers to the twelve states of Etruria and their governors, known as **lucumones.**

l. 476. **quam . . . ostentat.** Order for translation : **salutem quam inopina fors ostentat.**

l. 477. **fatis poscentibus,** abl. absol., ' destiny summoning thee ' =' at destiny's summons '.

te adfers, ' thou betakest thyself ' =' thou dost come '.

ll. 478, 9. **haud . . . sedes.** Order for translation : **haud procul hinc, fundata vetusto saxo, incolitur** (' there is inhabited ')

sedes urbis Agyllinae. The latter is known sometimes as **Agylla,** sometimes as **Caere.**

l. 479. **Lydia gens,** ' the Lydian race '. There was a strong tradition in the ancient world that the Etruscans came originally from Asia Minor—a view that now seems to be endorsed by most modern scholars. Lydia was a part of Asia Minor : hence **Lydius** is used by Vergil to denote the country of which Lydia is only a part.

l. 480. **iugis Etruscis,** local abl. ' on the Etruscan heights '.

ll. 481, 2. **hanc florentem** (**urbem** to be supplied) is the object of **tenuit,** but may be taken first and the present participle rendered by a pluperfect tense as the following **deinde** suggests : i.e. ' this city which had flourished for so many years,[1] king Mezentius next possessed . . .'

l. 483. **quid memorem,** ' why should I relate '. Note the meaning of **quid** and the translation of **memorem**—a deliberative subjunctive.

l. 484. **di . . . reservent,** ' may the gods keep (such treatment) for the head of himself (=for his own head) and for his family '. **reservent,** present subj. (optative, expressing a wish for the future).

l. 485. **quin etiam,** ' nay even '. Note this meaning of **quin** with the indicative.

l. 486. **componens** . . . Ignore the first -**que,** which really means ' both '.

l. 487. **tormenti genus.** The latter word is acc., in apposition to the whole preceding sentence, and exclamatory, ' a (monstrous) kind of torture! '

ll. 487, 8. **et sanie . . . necabat,** ' and in (that) foul embrace, dripping with gore and corruption, he slew them thus by a lingering death '.

l. 489. **infanda furentem,** ' (him) raging impiously '. **infanda** is actually acc. pl. neut. of the adjective, understood to qualify

---

[1] And still did so ; hence the present participle in Latin.

the noun which may be considered to be *implied* in **furere, ' to rage '**, i.e. ' to rage a rage '.

infanda furere, then =' to rage impious (rages) '. This is a form of the cognate accusative.

Finally we can translate the two words ' impious madman '.

l. 491. **ignem**, ' fire ' =' fire-brands '.

l. 492. **Rutulorum.** This gen. depends upon **agros.**

l. 493. **confugere, defendier** are historic infinitives, to be translated as perfect indics. **defendier** is an old form of the present infinitive passive.

hospitis, ' host ', not ' guest '.

l. 495. **praesenti Marte**, ' with instant war '. For **Mars** = ' war ', see the note on l. 181.

l. 496. **his ego . . . addam**, ' to these in-their-thousands, I shall appoint thee, Aeneas, (as) leader '.

l. 497. **toto namque . . . puppes.** Note : (i) **toto litore**, local abl., ' on all the . . . (ii) **puppes**, part for the whole,[1] ' sterns ' for ' ships '. In any case, we should expect Vergil to say that the crews ' **fremunt** ' rather than the ships.

l. 498. **signa ferre**, ' (them) advance the standards '.

retinet. Supply ' but ' before this verb and ' them ' as the object.

l. 499. **Maeoniae . . . iuventus.** For **Maeonia** (=Lydia), see the note on l. 479, and for the translation of **iuventus** on l. 105.

l. 500. **flos . . . virum**, lit. ' the flower and valour of men of old ' =' the valorous flower of an ancient race '.

l. 502. **fas.** Supply **est. nulli** is dat. with **Italo.**

l. 506. **Tarcho**, nom. Tarcho, or Tarchon, is an Etruscan, and leader of the Etruscan revolt against Mezentius.

l. 507. **succedam, capessam**, indirect command, dependent upon the idea of exhortation implied in the verbs **misit, mandat.** Supply in the translation ' urging that . . .'

ll. 508, 9. **sed mihi . . . vires.** The singular verb **invidet** has

---

[1] Synecdoche.

two subjects, senectus and **vires. tarda gelu,** 'sluggish with cold '='sluggish and chilled '.

mihi is dat. dependent upon **invidet,** '. begrudge (to) me the command '.

serae ... vires, lit. 'strength (too) late for brave (deeds) ' ='strength now too feeble for deeds of valour '.

l. 510. **exhortarer ni traheret,** 'I should exhort, did he not draw '. The imperfect subj. is used in conditional clauses which are suppositions contrary to present fact.

mixtus matre Sabella, lit. 'mixed, his mother (being) Sabine ' ='of mixed blood, having a Sabine mother '.

hinc, lit. 'hence ' ='from her ', i.e. 'from his mother '. Latin often uses adverbs to refer to people.

Evander is not disparaging the martial qualities of the Sabine race, but pointing out that as his son is partly of Italian stock, he is not qualified by the terms of the prophecy to lead the Etruscan army. See l. 503, **externos optate duces.**

l. 513. **ingredere,** lit. 'enter '. The verb needs to be expanded as follows : 'enter (upon thy destined work) '.

Teucrum, Italum, gen. pl.

l. 514. **hunc Pallanta.** Note : (i) this use of **hic** to point to someone present, 'Pallas here '. (ii) **Pallanta,** Greek acc. sg. ending, 3rd declension.

nostri, lit. 'of us '. But translate by 'my '.

ll. 515–17. **sub te ... annis.** Begin with **adsuescat,** 'let him learn ', jussive subj., as is **miretur** following.

sub te magistro, 'under thee (as) master ', i.e. 'under thy guidance '.

l. 518. **Arcadas,** adj., acc. pl. (Greek ending) in agreement with **equites.**

robora pubis lecta, 'the choice flower of our youth '. **robur** literally means 'hard-wood ' and especially 'oak '.

l. 519. **Pallas.** Supply **dabit,** 'will give '.

suo munere, 'on his own account '.

l. 520. **defixique . . . tenebant,** ' and kept their gaze down-cast '. The logical thing for Vergil to have written was **defixa ora tenebant.** With a disregard of strict grammar that other poets, no less than Vergil, often display, the participle has been made to agree with the masc. pl. subject instead.

l. 521. **Anchisiades.** Anchises was the father of Aeneas. He had accompanied his son in his wanderings in the Eastern Mediterranean and died before Aeneas was driven to N. Africa.

Achates. Achates in the Aeneid is the type of the faithful and loyal friend.

ll. 522, 3. **multaque . . . aperto,** ' and they were pondering on many a peril in their own sad hearts, had not Venus given . . .'

Note that the real apodosis ' and would have continued ', to the protasis **ni . . . dedisset,** has been suppressed although it can easily be understood from **putabant.** The genuine apodosis would have had its verb in the pluperfect subj.

aperto. It is not natural to have thunder and lightning when the sky is ' cloudless '. Hence the phenomenon is regarded as supernatural.

l. 524. **improviso** is an adv., ' unforeseen '.

vibratus . . . fulgor, lit. ' a flash darted from heaven '. Retain the Latin order and say, ' hurled from heaven a flash came . . .'

cum, ' with '.

l. 525. **visa.** Supply **sunt,** ' seemed '. **omnia** is the subject.

l. 526. **Tyrrhenusque.** Note : (i) **Tyrrhenus** goes in grammar with **clangor,** in sense with **tubae.** Translate as if you had **Tyrrhenae.** (ii) **mugire,** historic infinitive.

l. 528. **inter nubem,** ' through the veil of heaven '. The sky seems to the watchers to divide in order to reveal the arms to Aeneas and his friends. **nubes** could hardly mean ' cloud ', unless we wish to make Vergil give us an inconsistent picture.

caeli depends upon **regione serena.**

ll. 528, 9. **arma . . . rutilare . . . tonare,** ' they see arms gleam red and, clashed, thunder (=clash together thunderously) '. **pulsa** is the perf. part. pass. from **pello,** ' having been clashed '.

l. 531. **promissa,** pl. for sg., ' the promise '. Although this promise has not been mentioned by Vergil before, we can assume what it is from ll. 534, 5.

l. 532. **ne vero, ne quaere.** Note once again this verse construction for the prose **noli quaerere. profecto** is an adv. meaning ' indeed '. English, however, enforces an imperative, not with an adverb, but with ' I pray '.

l. 533. **poscor,** ' I am summoned '. If we place a full-stop after **poscor** as the Oxford Classical Text does, **Olympo** belongs to the next verb **missuram** and means ' from Olympus '.

If, however, we follow those editors who place the full-stop after **Olympo,** the latter is dat. of the agent ' by Heaven '. Cf. the note on l. 169. The fact that this dat. is found chiefly with the *perfect* passive is an argument in favour of the first punctuation.

l. 534. **Olympo . . . creatrix.** Order for translation : **diva creatrix cecinit (se) missuram (esse) hoc signum Olympo.**

l. 535. **Volcania,** not ' of Vulcan ', but ' fashioned by Vulcan '.

l. 536. **auxilio** is a dat. of purpose, ' for a help ', i.e. ' to help me '.

l. 538. **quam multa,** ' how many ', is used for the more common **quot.**

l. 540. **Thybri,** voc., as is **pater.**

poscant, rumpant, jussive subj., ' let them demand war . . .' **acies** is acc. pl.

l. 541. **se tollit,** ' he raises himself ' = the English intransitive, ' he rises '.

l. 542. **Herculeis ignibus,** ' with fire from Hercules' altar ', i.e. from the Ara Maxima in the valley.

l. 543. **hesternum . . . penates:** ' the Lar of yesterday and the tiny household gods ' are those of Evander which Aeneas had worshipped the day before on his arrival at Evander's house.

l. 544. **laetus**, adj. for adv., ' joyfully '. **adire** is the regular verb for ' approaching to worship '.

l. 546. **post**, adv. ' afterwards '. **hinc**, lit. ' hence '(= ' next ') goes with **graditur**, the subject of which is Aeneas.

ll. 547, 8. **quorum de numero . . . legit**, ' from whose number he chooses the outstanding in valour to follow him to battle '. **virtute**, abl. of respect. **qui . . . sequantur**, purpose or final subj.

l. 548. **pars . . . aqua**, ' the rest (**pars cetera**) glide down-the stream (**prona aqua**) '. The latter is abl. of route.

l. 549. **segnis**, adj. for adv., ' idly '. **secundo amni**, ' on the favouring current '.

l. 550. **nuntia . . . patrisque**, lit. ' to come (as) messenger to Ascanius of the fortunes and of his father '.
Note : (i) **ventura**, fut. part. in agreement with **pars cetera**. (ii) **rerumque patrisque**, a hendiadys for ' the fortunes of his father '.

l. 551. **dantur**, i.e. by Evander.

l. 552. **exsortem**. Supply **equum**, ' a picked steed '.

l. 553. **obit totum**, ' covers wholly '.

l. 554. **Fama . . .** Order for translation : **subito vulgata** (' spreading ') **per parvam urbem volat fama . . .**

l. 555. **equites ire**, acc. and infin., ' that . . .' **Tyrrheni regis**. The Etruscan king is Tarcho. **ad limina**, ' to the doors ', i.e. the horsemen are seeking Tarcho in his house.

l. 556. **propiusque . . . timor**, lit. ' nearer to peril goes fear ', i.e. ' closer upon peril treads fear '.

l. 558. **dextram euntis**, ' the hand of (him) going ', i.e. ' the hand of his departing son '.

l. 559. **inexpletus lacrimans**. **inexpletus** : adjective put for adverb is a common feature of Latin, and **inexpletus** may be rendered with **lacrimans**, ' weeping insatiably '.

l. 560. **O . . . annos**. Note that the present subj. expresses a wish *for the future* : ' O if only Jupiter would bring back . . .'

l. 561. **qualis eram.** Supply ' and make me such ' before these two words. Then **qualis** means ' as '.

l. 563. **sub,** ' down to '.

l. 564. **Feronia.** Feronia was an old Italian goddess whose worship was widely spread in Central Italy.

l. 565. **terna arma movenda,** ' three suits of arms to-be-wielded' obj. of **dederat.** His mother gave him three lives and three sets of arms in order that when once killed and stripped of arms, he might come to life with a fresh set.

Perhaps we might say for the gerundive **movenda,** ' for him to weild '.

l. 566. **ter . . . erat,** ' three times he was to-be-laid-low-in death ', i.e. ' he had to be laid low '.

cui, dat. after **abstulit,** ' from whom '.

l. 567. **armis,** abl. of separation in Latin : but we say, ' strip a person *of* his armour '.

l. 568. **non ego nunc divellerer,** ' I should not now be torn away '.

If we regard l. 560 as the protasis to this line, there seems to be an apparent irregularity, **si** with the present subj., followed in the apodosis by the imperfect subj.

If, however, we explain l. 560 as a wish for the future as was suggested in the notes, rather than as the strict protasis to l. 568, the irregularity disappears.

l. 569. **tuo,** with **amplexu** in the previous line.

l. 569. **finitimo huic capiti,** ' to this his neighbour's head '. Evander is referring, of course, to himself.

l. 570. **dedisset,** ' would have caused '.

l. 571. **viduasset** = **viduavisset.**

l. 573. **Arcadii regis,** gen. after **miserescite.** The Arcadian king is Evander, the speaker, who thus refers to himself.

l. 575. **incolumem Pallanta. incolumem** is proleptic, i.e. it gives the result of the verb **reservant.** See the note on l. 37.

fata. The ancient world seems to have believed that ' Fate ' was independent of the will of the gods and sometimes superior to it. In placing **fata** after **numina**, Vergil may be consciously referring to this belief.

l. 576. **visurus, venturus in unum**, future participles expressing purpose, ' to see ', ' to meet him '.

l. 577. **patior durare**, ' I have patience to endure '.

l. 579. **liceat.** Supply **mihi** and note the pres. subj. expressing a wish for the future : ' may it be allowed to me ', i.e. ' may I '.

l. 580. **dum** . . . Supply **sunt** as the verb twice.

ll. 582, 3. **gravior neu . . . vulneret**, ' nor may heavier tidings wound my ears '. **vulneret** is the same subj. as **liceat** in l. 579. A second wish or command if negative is always introduced by **neu** or **neve** instead of **ne**. In English we should prefer to say, for ' nor may . . .', ' and may no heavier . . .'

To appreciate fully the pathos of these beautiful lines, which are so characteristic of Vergil, read the synopsis of the epic in the Introduction, pp. xiv–xx, especially of Books X and XII.

l. 583. **digressu supremo**, ' at their last parting '.

l. 585. **iamque adeo.** **adeo** is often used as an enclitic in Latin to emphasise words : ' and *now* '.

l. 588. **pictis.** Look up **pingo**. **conspectus**, ' conspicuous '.

l. 589. **qualis.** The correlative **talis** has to be supplied in apposition with **Pallas**, ' (of such a kind) as '. Render, however, by ' even as '.

unda, local abl., ' in the wave '.

l. 590. **quem . . . ignes.** Translate this relative clause immediately after **Lucifer.** Then go on with **perfusus unda Oceani** and l. 591.

l. 591. **caelo**, local abl., ' in the . . .'

l. 594. **olli** is an old form of **illi** : nom. pl. masc.

qua . . . viarum, lit. ' where the goal of their journeys (is) nearest ', i.e. by the nearest way to their goal '.

l. 595. **it**, ' there rises '. **agmine facto**, lit. ' a column having been formed ' : render by a finite verb, ' a column is formed ', and insert ' and ' before the following line.

l. 596. **quadripedante ... campum** is an onomatopoeic line, for the rhythm and sound imitate the noise of a galloping horse.

l. 597. **est ingens ... amnem.** Order for translation : **prope Caeritis** (gen. sg.) **gelidum amnem est** (' there is ') **ingens lucus.**

l. 598. **religione . . . sacer,** ' widely reverenced by the piety of earlier generations ' (lit. ' of the fathers ').

l. 599. **inclusere.** Supply **eum** (=**lucum**) as the object.

nigra abiete, sing. for plural, ' with dark fir-trees '. **nemus** is acc.

l. 600. **fama est,** ' (there) is a story ', is followed by acc. and infin. **veteres Pelasgos sacrasse** (=**sacravisse**). The object of the latter is **lucumque diemque,** the first -que meaning ' both '.

The ancients called ' Pelasgian ' all the aboriginal populations of the Mediterranean basin.

l. 602. **qui ... Latinos.** This relative clause will be best rendered immediately after its antecedent **veteres Pelasgos.** The mood is indic., although the clause is dependent on a word in the indirect statement, because it is an addition given by Vergil, not a part of the original report.

l. 603. **tuta locis,** ' secure by reason of its site.' **locis,** abl. of cause.

l. 605. **legio,** ' host ', not ' legion '. **legio** literally means a ' levy '. **tendebat,** ' was encamped '.

l. 606. **bello,** ' for war ', with **lecta.**

l. 607. **corpora,** ' their bodies ', i.e. ' themselves '.

l. 608. **inter,** the prep. governs **aetherios nimbos.**

dea candida is in apposition with **Venus.**

ll. 609, 910. **natumque ... vidit.** Order for translation : **ut procul vidit natum secretum in reducta valle egelido flumine** (' by a cool stream ').

l. 611. **ultro.** No single word in English quite corresponds to this Latin word. It suggests that the statement it accompanies is an unexpected one. In this line, for example, Venus appeared visibly to her son, although such a manifestation on her part could hardly be expected. Translate by 'actually'.

ll. 612, 13. **en perfecta . . . munera.** Order for translation: **en munera perfecta promissa arte mei coniugis.**

munera here means 'gifts'.

l. 613. **ne dubites,** 'so that thou mayest not hesitate'.

l. 615. **amplexus,** acc. pl., and plural for sing.

l. 616. **sub adversa quercu,** 'under an oak facing (him)'.

l. 618. **per singula,** 'over each piece (of armour)'.

ll. 619, 20. **miraturque . . . vomentem,** 'and he wonders at, and turns over in his hands and arms the helmet . . .'

terribilem cristis, 'terrible with its plumes'.

l. 621. **ex aere,** 'of bronze' ='brazen'.

l. 622. **sanguineam,** 'blood-red'. The adjective refers with considerable exaggeration to the colour of the bronze.

qualis cum, '(such) as when' ='even as when'.

In this simile, which Vergil has borrowed from a Greek epic poet, Apollonius Rhodius, the bronze of the breastplate corresponds to the dark-blue cloud (**caerula nubes**) and the highlights on the metal to the sun's rays that make the cloud glow and gleam afar (**inardescit longeque refulget**).

l. 624. **lēves** means 'smooth': cf. **lĕvis,** 'light'.

ocreas. Greaves were worn on the legs to protect the shins. These greaves were made of electrum and gold 'smelted again and again' (**recocto**), i.e. 'refined'.

ll. 626–9. **illic . . . bella.** Begin with l. 626, then take **igni-potens fecerat,** then the phrases in apposition **haud vatum ignarus -que inscius venturi aevi.** The remaining words follow quite naturally.

res Italas, lit. 'Italian things' ='the story of Italy'.

haud vatum ignarus, lit. 'not ignorant of prophets' ='not ignorant of prophecy'. **haud** is carried on with **inscius**; therefore **-que** should be translated by 'or'.

aevi venturi, 'of the age to come'.

1. 629. ab Ascanio ' (to descend) from Ascanius '. **in ordine,** lit. ' in order ', i.e. ' one after the other '.

In describing this shield of Aeneas, Vergil is following a common practice of ancient poets, who often introduce into their compositions a description of a work of art. Homer, for example, had given in the Iliad (XVIII, 478 ff.) a full description of the shield of the Greek prince Achilles, on which were represented many common scenes of human life and its varied activities, in the city, in the country, in peace and war. Vergil uses Homer as a model, but relates the themes on the shield of Aeneas to the main purpose of his epic, viz. to glorify the Roman character and its imperial achievements, just as in Book VI he had used a Greek philosophical belief as a means of introducing to Aeneas and hence to generations of readers of his work a series of striking episodes from Roman history.

In these lines, therefore, every scene that the poet describes is, so to speak, a foreshadowing of famous events in Roman history from the suckling of the twins, Romulus and Remus, by the she-wolf, right down to Vergil's own day and the achievements of his patron, Augustus.

Some editors have suggested that in some of these scenes Vergil may well have had in mind certain works of art he had seen and appreciated, for some of the subjects he handles were popular with painters and sculptors.

ll. 630, 1. fecerat . . . lupam, ' he had represented the mother-wolf (**fetam lupam**) lying in the green cave of Mars '. **fecerat procubuisse,** lit. ' caused . . . to have lain down '.

The cavern is the Lupercal, for which see the note on l. 343.

l. 631. ubera circum, i.e. **circum ubera. huic** : translate this dat. by ' her ', and see the note on l. 160.

l. 632. ludere, lambere, mulcere, fingere. Translate these infinitives in the way suggested for **procubuisse** in l. 631, i.e. by present participles. Insert ' and ' between your translation of **ludere** and **pendentes.**

matrem is the object of **lambere.**

l. 633. **tereti cervice reflexa,** ' her shapely neck bent back '.

l. 634. **alternos,** ' (them) in turn '.

ll. 635–7. **nec procul . . .**   Begin with **addiderat,** l. 637.

raptas . . . Sabinas, ' the Sabine women lawlessly carried off '.

consessu . . . actis, lit. ' from the theatre's seated-throng, the great Circensian-games being held ', i.e. ' from the audience seated in the theatre when the . . . were being held '.
Note : (i) **consessus,** lit. ' a sitting together ', used in a concrete sense for ' the people seated together '. (ii) **actis,** perf. part. pass., used in the meaning of the present part. pass., which is wanting in Latin.

As the newly-founded city of Romulus grew in size, he failed to gain wives for his men from the neighbouring tribes, who were said to be very suspicious of the power of the rapidly-growing city, and he, therefore, resorted to the stratagem described in the text, by means of which he carried off the Sabine women who had assembled in Rome with their families to watch the games. The latter are said by Livy (I, 12) to be the Consualia, ' feast of Consus ', an old Roman god of agriculture. Actually the great Circensian games were instituted much later than the time of Romulus. The story of the ' rape of the Sabine women ' and their success in stopping the war which later broke out between their fathers and newly acquired husbands is one of the best-known of the early Roman legends and one which has attracted many European artists. See especially Rubens' painting in the National Gallery, London.

This famous story is aetiological, i.e. it is a story invented later to explain an early custom or tradition : in this case, we are given a precedent for the force put upon a bride before she entered her husband's home.

l. 637. **subitoque . . .,** ' and the sudden rising of a fresh war between the sons of Romulus and . . .'

Tatio. Tatius was a king of the Sabines ; **Cures,** one of their most important towns. Vergil is obviously using the name of the town for the people.

l. 639. **post**, adverb, ' afterwards '.   **idem**, nom. pl., in agreement with **reges**.

inter se is to be taken with **iungebant foedera**, ' made alliance with each other ' (lit. ' among themselves ').

l. 641. **caesa porca**, abl. absol., ' a sow having been sacrificed ', i.e. ' with the sacrifice of a sow '.

l. 642. **in diversa**, ' in opposite directions ', with **distulerant**.

l. 643. **at tu . . . maneres**, ' but thou, O Alban, shouldst have stood by thy words '. **maneres**, past jussive, =**debebas manere**.

dictis is a kind of local ablative.

Mettus Fufetius was a king of Alba and an ally of the Romans, who tried to betray them in battle by deserting them. He was punished in this cruel way by the Romans.

l. 646. **Porsenna iubebat**. Supply ' the Romans ' as the object. **Tarquinium eiectum**, ' the banished Tarquin ', is the object of **accipere**.

Tarquin, surnamed ' the Proud ', was, so legend tells us, the seventh and last king of the Romans. His arrogance and cruelty drove the nobles under the leadership of L. Junius to expel him in 509 B.C. and establish the republic.

Porsenna was the king of the Etruscans, and was anxious to restore Tarquinius to his throne as his family seems to have been of Etruscan origin.

l. 648. **Aeneadae**, ' the sons of Aeneas ' = ' the Romans ' here.

ll. 649, 50. **illum . . . aspiceres**. Order for translation : **aspiceres illum similem indignanti -que similem minanti**.

aspiceres, potential subj., ' thou couldst have seen '.

illum, i.e. Porsenna.

ll. 650, 1. **pontem . . .** Horatius Cocles (' One-eyed ') was the famous hero who barred the passage over the Sublician bridge to the invading forces of Porsenna until the Romans behind him had time to demolish it and thus save the city.

He is said to have swum across the Tiber to the Roman bank, in spite of his heavy armour and serious wounds.

Some scholars believe that in this legend we have another example of an aetiological story ; for opposite the Sublician bridge there was a statue of a lame, one-eyed man, who was not the hero Horatius, but the fire-god Vulcan.

auderet, innaret are subjunctive because they are in virtual oratio obliqua, i.e. the sentences represent the thoughts of Porsenna, ' because, as he perceived, Cocles dared . . .'

Cloelia was a Roman girl who had been given to Porsenna as a hostage. She broke her bonds (**vinclis ruptis**) and swam back to Rome, and when restored to the Etruscan king as he demanded, she so aroused his admiration for her exploit that he at once returned her to her city and family.

l. 652. **in summo,** ' at the top (of the shield) '.

l. 653. **Capitolia celsa,** ' the lofty Capitol ', pl. for sing.

Marcus Manlius was consul in 392 B.C. and defender of the Capitol in 387 B.C., when the Gauls who had defeated the Roman army at the Allia were in possession of the rest of the city. A surprise night attack by the Gauls upon the Capitol was foiled by the cackling of the sacred geese, which awakened Manlius and enabled him and his garrison to repulse the invaders.

For this exploit Manlius was surnamed Capitolinus. Scholars again see in the version we have given of this famous story an aetiological myth to explain this surname which belonged to a branch of the Manlii family.

l. 654. **Romuleoque . . . culmo,** ' and the palace of Romulus was rough with fresh thatch '. In the translation we have two examples of transferred epithets, for **Romuleo** (in grammar with **culmo**) has been taken with **regia,** and **recens** (in grammar with **regia**) has been taken with **culmo.**

The Romans seem to have maintained right down to Vergil's time on the Capitol and the Palatine ' a palace of Romulus ', i.e. a hut which they constantly kept newly thatched.

l. 655. **hic,** adverb, ' here '.

auratis, ' of gold ', with **porticibus** : **argenteus,** ' of silver ', with **anser.** Vergil is referring to the precious metals in which the reliefs were wrought on the shield.

l. 658. **tenebris, noctis opacae.** The attack on the citadel was made, so Livy [1] says, **nocte sublustri,** ' on a night when there was but little light '.

l. 659. **ollis** =illis, and is to be translated by a possessive adj., ' their '. ' Golden their locks . . .'

aurea. See the note on l. 655.

l. 661. **auro,** ' with gold ', i.e. with the gold necklet which was often worn by Gauls and Germans.

duo Alpina gaesa, ' two Alpine darts '. **gaesum** is a Gallic word for a type of spear peculiar to the Gauls.

protecti corpora, either ' protecting their limbs '—an instance of the Latin passive used in the sense of the Greek middle and therefore having a direct object (for which see the note on l. 286), or ' protected as to their limbs ', in which translation **corpora** is an acc. of respect.

Long shields are distinctive of the Gauls.

ll. 663–5. **hic . . .** Begin with **extuderat** (from **extundo**).

Salios. The word is connected with **salio,** ' leap ', and the priests were so named from their practice of honouring the god with ritual dances.

nudos Lupercos. The festival of the Lupercalia was held in Rome on Feb. 15th. It was customary for young men, naked except for girdles made from the skins of the sacrificed victims (goats and a dog) to run about the bounds of the Palatine city and strike those they met, especially women (to induce fertility) with the goat-skins. The festival seems to have combined purificatory and fertility rites, and beating of the bounds. See also the note on ll. 343, 4, and cf. Shakespeare's Julius Caesar, Act I, Sc. 2, ll. 1–10.

lapsa ancilia caelo, ' the shields fallen from heaven '. According to legend a shield (the ancile) fell from heaven as a token from the gods of goodwill towards Rome. To prevent the

[1] V. 47.

theft of so sacred a talisman, eleven copies, indistinguishable from the original, were made, and these ancilia were in the care of the Salii.

apices. The **apex** was a kind of cap worn by priests, its wooden peak adorned with a tuft of wool.

l. 665. **sacra,** ' the sacred vessels '.

l. 666. **pilentis in mollibus.** Before the capture of the important town of Veii in 395 B.C., Camillus, the victorious Roman general, vowed a tenth of the spoil to Apollo. When there was difficulty in fulfilling the vow after the fall of the town, the Roman matrons offered gold and all their jewellery to the treasury. In gratitude the senate gave them the honour of riding at sacred processions in **pilenta.**

hinc procul, ' away from these ' ; lit. ' afar off hence '.

l. 667. **Tartareas sedes . . .** ' The abode of Hades ' was ruled over by Dis or Pluto.

Vergil now gives us two scenes from the underworld in which appear Catiline, as the representative of the most sacrilegious of traitors, and Cato, as the ideal national hero.

l. 668. **minaci . . . scopulo,** ' hanging from a frowning cliff '.

Catiline was a profligate and bankrupt Roman aristocrat. Failing to obtain political office by constitutional methods, Catiline formed a conspiracy of men like himself and all the discontented to overthrow the state by a *coup d'état.* Vigorous counter-measures by the consul Cicero in 63 B.C. prevented the rising from being successful and gained for their author universal applause and the honorary title of **pater patriae,** ' father of his country '.

Furiarum. The idea of the ' avenging spirits ' or ' Furies ' is borrowed by Vergil from Greek tragedy, where they relentlessly pursue those who have committed unnatural murder. Catiline will come under this class as he had been guilty of **impietas** towards his fatherland. Hence the Romans called traitors **parricidae,** lit. ' father-slayers '.

l. 670. **secretosque pios,** ' and, set apart, the good '.

There were many famous Catos in Roman history. Their

family had the reputation of being serious, conservative, and morose. Vergil is referring here to the Cato who was a contemporary of Julius Caesar and who refused to survive the destruction of the republic by the famous Roman general. He committed suicide in N. Africa, and won for himself an undying fame as one who refused to betray his principles and compromise his position.

It is important to remember that, as Vergil and his contemporaries conceived it, the underworld to which all men went at death was highly complex and divided into different quarters for different types of sinners. The good, however, dwelt in the Elysian Fields, and Vergil has placed Cato among the blessed (**pii**) who ' live ' there.

l. 671. **haec inter** =**inter haec,** ' amid these (scenes) '—an example of anastrophe. Vergil seems to have placed the scenes he has already described on the rim of the shield. He is now going to give us what must have been the centre-piece —a description of the sea-fight off Actium between Octavianus (Augustus) and Antony and Cleopatra (31 B.C.).

ibat, ' stretched '.

l. 672. **aurea,** ' wrought in gold '.

caerula, neut. pl. of the adj. used as a noun, ' the blue (of the sea) '.

cano, from **cānus.**

l. 673. **circum,** adv., ' all around '.

argento clari, ' glittering in silver ' =' of glittering silver ' **in orbem,** ' in circles '.

ll. 675, 6. **in medio ... erat.** Order for translation : **in medio erat cernere** (' it was possible to see ') **aeratas classes, Actia bella.** The use of **esse** in this sense is imitated from Greek.

Actia bella, ' the fight off Actium '. The latter is a promontory at the entrance to the Ambracian gulf on the west coast of Greece.

In the closing lines of this book, Vergil gives us four scenes from the exploits of Augustus. The first is the battle of Actium (ll. 675–706).

l. 676. **totumque . . . Leucaten,** ' and thou couldst have seen all Leucate stirring with warlike preparation ' (lit. ' war prepared ').

For **videres,** see the note on l. 650.

Leucaten is the Greek acc. of Leucate, a cape at the southern end of Leucas, an island near Actium.

l. 677. **fervere** is a dactyl, as Vergil is using the infinitive of an older form (3rd conj.) of the verb. Cf. **effulgere** in the same line. For the acc. and infin. here, corresponding to English accus. and participle, cf. previous instances in ll. 631, 2, 4, 7.

fluctus, acc. pl., and subject of the infinitive **effulgere.** Note the 3rd conj. infin. of this verb, which gives Vergil the dactyl he needs in the 5th foot.

l. 678. **hinc,** ' on one side '. **Augustus Caesar :** Octavianus was actually the great-nephew of Julius Caesar, who made him his heir in his will. In 27 B.C., four years after the battle of Actium, he had the title Augustus conferred upon him. His adopted name Caesar became an official title for all succeeding Roman emperors and has found its way into modern Europe as ' Czar ' and ' Kaiser '.

l. 679. **cum patribus . . . dis.** Note : (i) the spondee in the 5th foot instead of the customary dactyl. (ii) **penatibus et magnis dis,** which may be a hendiadys, ' with the great gods, the Penates ' or ' with the Penates and the great gods ', the latter being images of such major divinities as Jupiter, Juno, contrasted with localised gods such as those peculiar to a household or a city.

Notice that in these two lines Augustus is represented as leading Italians (not Asiatics and Egyptians as Antony was) into battle, and that he has on his side all that is truly Roman, the fathers = (the senate), the people, and the household gods. On Antony's side there was all that was truly un-Roman, a woman (Cleopatra) who it was said aspired to be the queen of Rome, effeminate Asiatics and half-breeds. Cf. lines 685–688.

l. 680. **stans.** Translate the present participle by ' stands ', ending the sentence at **puppi.** Begin a fresh sentence with **cui,**

the dative being equivalent to the Englih possessive adj. ' his '
(with **tempora**, ' temples ').

geminas flammas, ' two rays (of light) '.

l. 681. **patriumque . . . sidus**, ' and his father's star is re-
vealed on his head '. His father is his adopted one, Julius
Caesar.

l. 682. **parte alia**, ' elsewhere '. Agrippa was one of the most
successful of the generals and admirals of Augustus. Later he
became his son-in-law.

Agrippa. Supply est.

l. 683. **arduus** =stans celsa in puppi of l. 680 : translate, ' in
his lofty ship ', (lit. ' towering ').

cui, ' his ' with **tempora** in the next line.

belli insigne superbum, ' proud badge of war ', is a
phrase loosely in apposition with the rest of the sentence. It
should be translated last.

l. 684. **navali rostrata corona**, lit. ' beaked with the naval
crown ' =' ringed by the beaked naval crown '.

The **corona rostrata** is a diadem with the triple beak of a
quinquereme in the middle of the forehead. Agrippa, who
received this decoration in 36 B.C. for his victory over the
pirates of Sextus Pompeius, is said to have been the first
person to have been thus honoured.

l. 685. **hinc**, ' on the other side '. Cf. **hinc**, l. 678.

ope barbarica, ' with barbarian aid ' : Antony's army was
said to contain contingents from every quarter of the East.

l. 686. **victor**, ' victorious '. **litore rubro**. ' The Red Sea '
in the Ancient World included the Indian Ocean and the
Persian Gulf, besides the Red Sea proper as we know it, and,
moreover, the coasts that these seas washed.

l. 688. **sequiturque . . . coniunx**, ' and (there) follows (O
impious shame!) his Egyptian bride '.

Augustus had certainly made the best use for propaganda
purposes of the liaison between Antony and Cleopatra. Rum-
ours were circulated in Rome that Antony was setting himself

up as a king on the eastern model, and was preparing to bring his lover as his queen to rule over the Roman Empire. To the Roman as to the Greek, eastern nations were barbarians, effeminate and definitely inferior to the people of the west. One needs little imagination to picture the strong feeling aroused in Rome at the thought of Cleopatra's claiming to be the wife of a Roman citizen and, much worse, aiming at royal power.

Cf. the thirty-seventh ode of Horace, Book I, which he wrote after news of Cleopatra's death reached Rome in 30 B.C.

l. 689. **una** is an adverb.

ruere, spumare, historic infinitives.

reductis (with **remis**), ' pulled back ' (to the chests).

l. 690. **tridentibus.** The bows of ships seem to have been equipped with three iron prongs for ramming.

l. 691. **alta petunt. alta** is acc. pl. neut. object of **petunt** : ' depths ', or ' deep '. The subject of the verb is the ships of Antony's fleet.

credas, ' thou wouldst think '. Cf. **videres,** l. 676, and **aspiceres,** l. 650. Note that Vergil uses the present tense here.

ll. 691, 2. **pelago . . . altos,** ' thou wouldst think that the Cyclades, torn up (from their beds), were floating upon the sea and that with mountains lofty mountains clashed '.

Vergil is alluding to the ships of Antony's fleet, vast and unwieldy vessels.

l. 693. **tanta mole** ' in so great mass ' = ' in such massive ships '. **viri,** ' the seamen ', nom. pl.

The translation above refers the first phrase to Antony's ships, and the **turritis puppibus** (in dat. after **instant**) to those of Agrippa, for we know that he had equipped his ships with towers. Cf. **arduus** in l. 683, which seems again to refer to the towers which Agrippa used as fighting tops.

l. 694. **stuppea flamma,** lit. ' flame of tow ' = ' flaming tow '.

telis volatile ferrum, lit. ' iron flying in darts ' = ' flying darts of iron '.

manu, ' from their hands '.

It is possible to take **telis** = tormentis, ' from war engines ', and thus obtain a contrast with **manu.**

l. 695. **nova caede,** ' with fresh-(spilt) blood '.

l. 696. **regina.** ' The queen ' is Cleopatra. The **sistrum** with which she summons her troops was a kind of rattle, very much used in the worship of the Egyptian deity Isis to arouse religious excitement and enthusiasm.

l. 697. **geminos angues.** Cleopatra committed suicide when she realised that she would be unable to use Octavian (Augustus) to further her own ambitions as she had her previous lovers, Julius Caesar and Antony. As she believed she was the daughter of the Egyptian sun-god Re, she used the asp which was sacred to this deity as the instrument of her death. It is probable, therefore, that she believed that by employing this method of suicide she would most certainly return to her father, the sun-god.

l. 698. **omnigenum deum,** gen. pl. dependent upon **monstra.**

latrator Anubis. Anubis was one of the Egyptian gods of the dead and was represented on the monuments as a jackal.

In these lines Vergil represents the victory of Actium as the triumph of the old Roman gods over the foreign deities from the East which, frequently imported into Rome, were generally regarded as effeminate, unmanly and degrading.

l. 701. **caelatus ferro,** ' engraved in steel '.

Dirae = the Furies of l. 669. **ex aethere,** ' (swooping) from the heaven '.

l. 702. **scissa.** Look up **scindo,** and scan the line to find the length of the **a,** in order that you may determine whether the participle agrees with **Discordia** (nom.) or **palla** (abl.).

In Book VI, ll. 280, 1, Vergil places Discordia in Hades near the entrance along with many similar monstrous creatures. He describes her thus :

> **et Discordia demens,**
> **vipereum crinem vittis innexa cruentis.**
> ' and mad Discord,
> her snaky locks bound with blood-stained fillet.'

l. 704. **Actius Apollo.** After his victory, Augustus had instituted a quinquennial festival at Actium in honour of the god Apollo, for the sea-fight took place within sight of the god's temple on the promontory.

l. 705. **eo terrore,** ' at that terror ', i.e. of the archer-god's participating, in accordance with epic tradition, in the battle.

l. 706. **vertebant terga,** lit. ' turned their backs ' = ' turned and fled '.

The nationalities are not to be understood too literally. Vergil wishes to emphasise the heterogeneous character of the combatants that made up Antony's army, and he chooses those names which normally meant ' the east ' to a Roman reader.

ll. 707-13 introduce the second scene—the flight of Cleopatra.

ll. 707-8. **ipsa . . . funes,** ' the queen herself was seen to spread her sails to the winds she had invoked and now, even now, to slacken the sheets '.

funes are the ropes at the lower corners of the sails which are used to regulate the angle and extent of their exposure to the wind.

laxos is proleptic with **immittere:** literally ' to let the sheets go loose ' = ' to slacken '.

l. 709. **pallentem morte futura,** ' pale at her approaching doom '.

l. 709. **illam fecerat ignipotens ferri,** ' her the lord of fire had fashioned borne on . . .' For the infin. **ferri** thus translated cf. **fecerat procubuisse,** l. 631.

Iapyge. The ' Iapygian ' wind blows seaward from the heel of Italy, and is therefore a west-north-west wind—most favourable to Cleopatra in her flight to Egypt.

l. 711. **contra** is an adverb and means ' over against this ', i.e. in another part of the centre of the shield.

magno corpore, abl. of quality or description, ' of mighty frame '. **Nilum** is a second object of **fecerat,** l. 710.

l. 712. **sinus,** acc. pl., and pl. for sing.

tota veste, ' with all his vesture '. This phrase is possibly in reference to the wide delta of the Nile.

l. 713. **caeruleum** goes with **gremium.**

latebrosa flumina, lit. ' streams full of hiding-places '. This phrase perhaps contains a reference to the mystery of the Nile's source. We may render : ' into (**in**) the manifold refuge of his streams '.

victos is the object of **vocantem.**

ll. 714–19. These lines, the third scene, describe the triumph of Augustus at Rome.

l. 714. **invectus,** ' entering '. Note : (i) the passive of **veho** is used as a deponent in the meaning ' go '. (ii) the present tense in English : in Latin the perf. participle of deponent verbs is commonly used in a present significance.

triplici triumpho. The triumph is a triple one because Augustus had won victories at Actium, in Dalmatia, and at Alexandria.

Romana moenia, ' to the city of Rome ', acc. of the goal of motion.

l. 716. **maxima** = **magna.   ter centum delubra** is in apposition with **immortale votum** in the line before. **ter centum** is a round number, and Augustus is poetically conceived as consecrating all at once the temples he restored and repaired during his reign.   Such a religious policy was a deliberate attempt to restore the virtues and qualities which he and his advisers believed had made Rome great.

A great ode of Horace, the sixth of Book III, commemorates this part of the domestic policy of the emperor.   Ovid, too, addresses him as

templorum positor, templorum sancte repostor.[1]

l. 719. **stravere.**   Look up **sterno.**

l. 720. **ipse,** Augustus.   We now have, in ll. 720–8, the last scene, the emperor reviewing the gifts of the nations.

[1] Fasti II, 65.

E

candentis Phoebi, ' of the dazzling (temple of) Phoebus '.

Augustus erected this temple to Apollo on the Palatine in 24 B.C., and the material used was white (**niveo**) marble.

l. 721. **aptatque.**   The object is ' them ', i.e. the gifts.

l. 723. **quam variae ... armis,** lit. ' as diverse in tongues, so (diverse) in style of dress and arms ' = ' differing as much in style of dress and arms as in language '.

ll. 724–6. **hic Nomadum ... finxerat. hic** is an adverb. Begin with **Mulciber** (nom.) **finxerat** (verb).

There are, first, the Nomads of Numidia, a country to the west and, south of the city of Carthage, and the ' ungirt ' Africans, the latter apparently wearing no girdles.   These peoples are representative of the southernmost natives of the Roman Empire.   Next Vergil describes the homage of the East : the Leleges and Cares representing Asia Minor.   The Geloni were a Scythian people who lived in south Russia (the modern Ukraine) and, therefore, remind the poet's readers of the extension of the Roman Empire north-eastward.

The remaining lines take us from the Euphrates, which may be regarded as the limit of Roman influence in the east, to the Morini in northern Gaul and to the Rhine, the boundary between Roman Gaul and the German tribes to the east, then back to the Dahae, who lived by the Caspian Sea, and the Araxes, a river in Armenia (the modern Aras), which had recently had a bridge built over it by Augustus to replace one swept away by a flood, that had been made by Alexander.

By his artistic use of proper names, Vergil heightens the beauty and music of his lines and, at the same time, conveys to his readers a vivid picture of the extent and sweep of the Roman Empire.

l. 726. **Euphrates ... undis. ibat,** ' flowed '.   **iam ...undis,** lit. ' tamer now in respect of its waters ' = ' its waters tamer now '.   **undis,** abl. of respect.   In the period 22–19 B.C., Augustus visited Greece and Asia Minor and won a great diplomatic victory over the Parthians.

i. 727. **Rhenusque bicornis,** ' and the two-horned Rhine '.

See the note on l. 77. The poet may also be referring to the two mouths of the Rhine, the Rhine proper and the Waal.

l. 729. **dona parentis,** ' his mother's gift ', is in apposition to **talia,** object of **miratur,** of which the contained subject is Aeneas.

l. 730. **rerumque ignarus,** ' and (though) ignorant of the deeds '.

l. 731. **famamque . . . nepotum,** ' the fame and fortunes of his line (lit. descendants) '. This phrase is the object of **attollens.** What he actually lifts of course is the shield on which these things are represented.

VOCABULARY

N.B.—In the following vocabulary the figures (1), (2), (3), (4), after the verbs, denote the conjugation. No conjugation number is given in the case of -io verbs like *capio*.

ā (ab), *prep. with abl.*, from, by.

abiēs, -etis, *f.*, fir-tree, fir-wood.

abigō, -ere, -ēgī, -āctum (3), drive away.

abitus, -ūs, *m.*, departure.

abiūrō (1), deny on oath (263).

abrumpō, -ere, -rūpī, -ruptum (3), break off.

absistō, -ere, -stitī (3), cease.

absum, -esse, āfuī, be wanting *or* lacking (148) ; be absent.

ac, *see* atque.

accēdō, -ere, -cessī, -cessum (3), draw near, approach.

accendō, -ere, -ndī, -nsum (3), set on fire ; inflame (501).

accessus, -ūs, *m.*, approach, access.

accipiō, -ere, -cēpī, -ceptum, receive, welcome.

ācer, ācris, ācre, eager, fierce ; valiant (342, 441, 614).

ācernus, -a, -um, of maple wood.

acervus, -ī, *m.*, heap.

Achātēs, -ae, *m.*, Achates (*Trojan companion of Aeneas*).

aciēs, -eī, *f.*, line of battle.

Actius, -a, -um, of Actium.

acuō, -ere, -uī, -ūtum (3), sharpen.

acūtus, -a, -um, sharpened, keen.

ad, *prep. with acc.*, to, towards ; at.

addō, -ere, -didī, -ditum (3), add ; set (637).

adeō, -īre, -īvī *or* iī, -itum, go to, approach ; visit (302).

adeō, *adv.*, so much, so very.

adferō, -ferre, attulī, adlātum, bring to.

adfīgō, -ere, -xī, -xum (3), fasten to ; fix upon.

(adfor) -fārī, -fātus (1), *dep.*, speak to, address.

adhibeō (2), add to.

adhūc, *adv.*, still, as yet.

adiciō, -ere, -iēcī, -iectum, add.

adimō, -ere, -ēmī, ēmptum (3), take away.

adiungō, -ere, -iūnxī, -iūnctum (3), join to.

adlābor, -ī, -lapsus (3), *dep.*, glide towards.

adloquor, -ī, -locūtus (3), *dep.*, address.

adluō, -ere, -uī (3), wash.

adsiduē, *adv.*, assiduously, unremittingly.

adsuēscō, -ere, -suēvī, -suētum (3), become accustomed, accustom oneself (to) (174, 517).

adsum, -esse, -fuī, am at hand ; aid.

advehō, -ere, -xī, -ctum (3), carry to *or* towards ; *in pass.*, sail (11, 136).

adventus, -ūs, *m.*, arrival.

adversus, -a, -um, facing.

advertō, -ere, -tī, -sum (3), turn to ; attend, give heed (50).

advocō (1), summon ; call to one's aid (250).

aedēs, -is, *f.*, temple ; *in pl.*, house.

aegis, -idis, *acc.* aegida, *f.*, aegis.

Aegyptius, -a, -um, of Egypt.

Aegyptus, -ī, *f.*, Egypt.

Aeneadēs, -ae, *m.*, son *or* descendant of Aeneas ; Trojan ; =Roman (648).

Aenēās, -ae, *m.*, Aeneas.

aēnus, -a, -um, bronze *as adj.*

Aeolius, -a, -um, of Aeolus (*god of the winds*), said to dwell in the Aeolian islands between Italy and Sicily.

aequō (1), make equal.

aequor, -oris, *n.*, level surface ; water (89, 674) ; flood (96).

aerātus, -a, -um, bronze-beaked.

āĕrius, -a, -um, lofty.

aes, aeris, *n.*, bronze, copper.

aestuō (1), seethe, rage ; eddy (258).

aestus, -ūs, *m.*, tide, sea.

aetās, -ātis, *f.*, time (200), age (326).

aeternus, -a, -um, eternal, everlasting.

aethēr, -eris, *m.*, *acc.* -era, heaven, sky.

aetherius, -a, -um, in the heavens, ethereal.

Aetnaeus, -a, -um, of Etna.

aevum, -ī, *n.*, age (307) ; time (627).

Afer, -fra, -frum, African ; *as noun*, an African.

F

ager, agrī, *m.*, field, countryside, land.

āgmen, -inis, *n.*, column, (*of men*).

āgnōscō, -ere, -nōvī, -nitum (3) recognise.

agō, -ere, ēgī, āctum (3), drive ; se agere, be in motion, be stirring ; *imper.* age, agite, come !

agrestis, -e, *adj.*, *also as noun*, rustic, peasant.

Agrippa, -ae, *m.*, Agrippa (*general of Augustus*).

Agyllīnus, -a, -um, of Agylla (*Etruscan town*).

aiō, *defective vb.*, say.

āla, -ae, *f.*, wing.

Albula, -ae, *f.*, Albula (*old name of the Tiber*).

albus, -a, -um, white.

Alcīdēs, -ae, *m.*, son of Alceus, =Hercules.

āles, -itis, *adj.*, winged; *as noun, c.*, (*gen. pl.*, alituum) bird.

aliquandō, *adv.*, at last (200) ; once (602).

aliquis, -quid, someone, something.

alius, -a, -ud, other ; aliī . . . aliī, some . . . others.

almus, -a, -um, kindly, propitious.

alō, -ere, -uī, altum *or* alitum (3), nourish, sustain.

Alpīnus, -a, -um, Alpine.

altāria, -ium, *n. pl.*, altar.

alter, -era, -erum, one *or* the other (*of two*) ; second.

alternus, -a, -um, by turns.

altus, -a, -um, high (115), deep ; tall (162).

ambiguus, -a, -um, doubtful.

ambō, -ae, -ō, both.

amictus, -ūs, *m.*, dress, garment.

amīcus, -ī, *m.*, friend ; *as adj.*, friendly, gracious.

āmittō, -ere, -mīsī, -missum (3), lose.

amnis, -is, *m.*, river.

amoenus, -a, -um, pleasant, charming.

amor, -ōris, *m.*, love ; desire (163)

Amphitryōniadēs, -ae, *m.*, son of Amphitryon, i.e. Hercules.

amplector, -ī, -plexus (3), *dep.*, embrace.

amplexus, -ūs, *m.*, embrace.

an, *conj.*, *introducing second half of alternative indirect question*, or, or whether.

Anchīsēs, -ae, *m.*, Anchises (*father of Aeneas*).

Anchīsiadēs, -ae, *m.*, son of Anchises, *i.e.* Aeneas.

ancīle, -is, *n.*, sacred shield.

angō, -ere, ānxī (3), strangle.

anguis, -is, *m. and f.*, snake.

angustus, -a, -um, narrow.

anhelō (1), gasp, pant.

anima, -ae, *f.*, life (564), breath, wind.

animal, -ālis, *n.*, animal, living creature.

animus, -ī, *m.*, soul, spirit, mind ; *in pl.*, wrath (228).

annus, -ī, *m.*, year.

annuus, -a, -um, yearly.

ānser, -is, *m.*, goose.

ante, *prep. with acc.*, before ; *adv.*, before, first.

Antōnius, -ī, *m.*, Marcus Antonius.

antrum, -ī, *n.*, cave.

Anūbis, -is, (-idis), *m.* Anubis (*Egyptian deity*).

aperiō, -īre, -uī, -ertum (4), open, reveal.

apertus, -a, -um, open.

apex, -icis, *m.*, peak.

Apollō, -inis, *m.*, Apollo.

appāreō (2), appear, loom (557).

aptō (1), fit out ; hang (721).

apud, *prep. with acc.*, at, with, among.

aqua, -ae, *f.*, water.

aquōsus, -a, -um, watery.

āra, -ae, *f.*, altar.

Arabs, -bis, *m.*, Arab.

Araxēs, -is, *m.*, the Araxes (*modern Aras, river in Armenia*).

arbor, -oris, *f.*, tree.

Arcadia, -ae, *f.*, Arcadia.

Arcadius, -a, -um, Arcadian.

Arcas, -adis, *m.*, an Arcadian.

arceō (2), protect.

arcus, -ūs, *m.*, bow.

ardeō, -ēre, ārsī (2), burn, (*intr.*)

arduus, -a, -um, steep (417) towering (299).

argenteus, -a, -um, silver, *as adj.*

argentum, -ī, *n.*, silver.

Argīlētum, -ī, *n.*, Argiletum (*a district in Rome*).

Argolicus, -a, -um, of Argolis, *i.e.* Greek.

Argus, -ī, *m.*, Argus (*hundred-eyed guardian of Io*).

arma, -ōrum, *n. pl.*, arms, armour.

armentum, -ī, *n.*, cattle.

armō (1), arm, equip.

ars, artis, *f.*, craft, skill (226, 377) ; cunning (143).

artus, -ūs, *m.*, limb.

arvum, -ī, *n.*, field ; **Neptūnia arva** = the sea (695).

arx, arcis, *f.*, citadel.

asper, -era, -erum, rough, rude ;
fierce (330).

aspiciō, -ere, -spēxī, -spectum, behold, look upon.

aspīrō (1), breathe into.

ast, *conj.*, but.

astrum, -ī, *n.*, star.

asȳlum, -ī, *n.*, asylum, refuge
(*sanctuary instituted by Romulus*).

at, *conj.*, but.

āter, ātra, ātrum, black, gloomy.

Atlantis, -idis, *f.*, daughter of
Atlas.

Atlas, -ntis, *m.*, Atlas (*supported
the world upon his shoulders*).

atque, *conj.*, and.

Atrīdēs, -ae, *m.*, son of Atreus ;
name often given to the brothers
Agamemnon *and* Menelaus.

attollō, -ere (3), lift up, raise.

auctor, -ōris, *m.*, founder (134,
269).

audāx, -ācis, daring.

audeō, -ēre, ausus (2), *semi-dep.*,
dare.

audiō (4), hear, listen to.

auferō, -ferre, abstulī, ablātum,
take *or* bear away.

augeō, -ēre, auxī, auctum (2), increase, *trans.*

Augustus, -ī, *m.*, Augustus (*formerly Octavianus, nephew and
son by adoption of Julius
Caesar*).

aura, -ae, *f.*, air, breeze.

aurātus, -a, -um, gilded.

aureus, -a, -um, golden.

auris, -is, *f.*, ear.

Aurōra, -ae, *f.*, Aurora (*goddess of
the dawn*) : the dawn, East
(686).

aurum, -ī, *n.*, gold.

Ausonius, -a, -um, Italian.

Auster, -trī, *m.*, the South Wind.

aut, *conj.*, or ; aut . . . aut, either
. . . or.

autem, *conj.*, but, yet, however.

auxilium, -ī, *n.*, help, aid ; *in pl.*,
troops, forces.

āvellō, -ere, -vellī (vulsī), -vulsum
(3), tear *or* rend away.

Aventīnus, -ī, *m.*, the Aventine
(*one of the seven hills of Rome*).

āvertō, -ere, -tī, -sum (3), turn
away ; carry off (208).

axis, -is, *m.*, vault (*of heaven*).

Bacchus, -ī, *m.*, Bacchus (*god of
wine*).

Bactra, -ōrum, *n. pl.*, Bactra
(*modern Balkh, in Afghanistan*).

barathrum, -ī, *n.*, pit, gulf, chasm.

barbaricus, -a, -um, barbaric.

bellō (1), fight.

Bellōna, -ae, *f.*, Bellona (*goddess
of war*).

bellum, -ī, *n.*, war.

bicolor, -ōris, of two colours.

bicornis, -e, two-horned.

bidēns, -ntis, *f.* sheep (*lit. with two
teeth*).

bimembris, -e, of double shape.

bīnī, -ae, -a, *lit.* two each = two
(168).

birēmis, -is, *f.*, bireme.

bis, *adv.*, twice.

bōs, bōvis, *m. and f.*, ox, bull, cow.

bracchium, -ī, *n.*, arm.

Brontēs, -ae, *m.*, Brontes, ' the
Thunderer ' (*a Cyclops*).

Cācus, -ī, *m.*, Cacus.

cadāver, -eris, *n.*, corpse, carcase.

cadō, -ere, cecidī, cāsum (3), fall ; set (*of stars*).

caecus, -a, -um, dark.

caedēs, -is, *f.*, slaughter, gore ; murder (483).

caedō, -ere, cēcīdī, caesum (3), slaughter, slay.

caelō (1), engrave.

caelum, -ī, *n.*, heaven, sky.

Caere, *n.*, *indecl.*, *apart from gen. sg.* Caeritis, Caere (*town in Etruria*).

caeruleus, -a, -um, sea-blue, azure (713).

caerulus, -a, -um, dark, sea-blue, azure.

Caesar, -aris, Caesar, *a cognomen of the Julian clan.*

caesariēs, -eī, *f.*, locks.

calīgō, -inis, *f.*, gloom.

calor, -ōris, *m.*, heat.

camīnus, -ī, *m.*, furnace, forge.

campus, -ī, *m.*, plain, field.

candēns, -ntis, dazzling.

candidus, -a, -um, white ; fair (138, 608).

canis, -is, *c.*, dog.

canistrum, -ī, *n.*, basket (*of osier*).

canō, -ere, cecinī, cantum (3), sing ; prophesy.

cantus, -ūs, *m.*, song, chant (285) ; music.

cānus, -a, -um, white, (*of hair*).

capessō, -ere, -īvī, -ītum (3), lay hold of, take.

capiō, -ere, cēpī, captum, take ; receive (363) ; charm (311).

Capitōlium, -iī, *n.*, the Capitol (*temple of Jupiter on the Capitoline Hill*).

caput, -itis, *n.*, head.

carbasus, -ī, *f.*, fine linen, lawn.

Carēs. *acc.* -as, -um, *m. pl.*, the Carians (*natives of Caria in Asia Minor*).

carīna, -ae, *f.*, keel (*of ship*) ; ship.

Carīnae, -ārum, *f. pl.*, Carinae (*a district in Rome*).

carmen, -inis, *n.*, song.

Carmenta, -ae, *or* Carmentis, -is, *f.*, Carmenta (*a nymph, mother of Evander*).

Carmentālis, -e, of Carmenta.

cārus, -a, -um, dear, beloved.

castra, -ōrum, *n. pl.*, camp.

castus, -a, -um, chaste, pure.

cāsus, -ūs, *m.*, fall, hap ; mischance (578).

catēna, -ae, *f.*, chain, fetter.

caterva, -ae, *f.*, throng, troop.

Catilīna, -ae, *m.*, Catiline.

Catō, -ōnis, *m.*, Cato.

cauda, -ae, *f.*, tail.

causa, -ae, *f.*, cause ; plea (395).

cavea, -ae, *f.*, theatre.

caverna, -ae, *f.*, cavern, vault.

cavus, -a, -um, hollow.

cēdō, -ere, cessī, cessum (3), yield ; go (395).

celebrō (1), celebrate, honour.

celer, -is, -e, swift.

celerō (1), quicken, hasten.

celsus, -a -um, high, lofty.

centum, a hundred.

Cerēs, -eris, *f.*, Ceres (*goddess of agriculture*).

cernō, -ere, crēvī, crētum (3), perceive, discern.

certāmen, -inis, *n.*, contest, struggle.

certātim, *adv.*, emulously.

certus, -a, -um, sure, certain, assured.

cervīx, -īcis, *f.*, neck.

cēterus, -a, -um, other, remaining: the rest of.

Chalybes, -um, *m. pl.*, the Chalybes, *a people in Pontus.*

chalybs, -ybis, *m.*, steel.

chlamys, -ydis, *f.*, cloak.

chorus, -ī, *m.*, troop ; band (287, 718).

cieō, -ēre, cīvī, citum (2), rouse : summon (354).

cingō, -ere, -nxī, -nctum (3), encircle, wreathe.

cinis, -eris, *m.*, ashes.

Circēnsis, -e, of the Circus.

circum, *adv., and prep. with acc.*, around.

circumdō, -are, -dedī, -datum (1), place round, surround.

circumsistō, -ere, -stetī *or* -stitī, (3), surround.

circumsonō (1), fill with sound.

circumstō, -stāre, -stetī (1), encircle (300).

citus, -a, -um, swift.

cīvis, -is, *c.*, citizen.

clāmor, -ōris, *m.*, shout ; noise, clamour (216).

clangor, -ōris, *m.*, noise ; blare (526).

clārus, -a, -um, bright, famous.

classis, -is, *f.*, fleet.

claudō, -ere, -sī, -sum (3), shut ; bound (473).

clipeus, -ī, *m.*, shield.

Cloelia, -ae, *f.*, Cloelia.

Coclēs, -itis, ' one-eyed ' (*cognomen of Horatius*).

coeō, -īre, -īvī, -itum, come together, meet.

coepī, -isse, -tum, *defect. vb.*, began.

coeptum, -ī, *n.*, enterprise.

cōgnātus, -a, -um, kindred, related.

cōgnōmen, -inis, *n.*, surname, name.

cogō, -ere, coēgi, coāctum (3), collect, muster.

collis, -is, *m.*, hill.

collum, -ī, *n.*, neck.

colus, -ūs *or* -ī, *f.*, distaff.

coma, -ae, *f.*, hair, locks.

comes, -itis, *c.*, comrade, companion.

comitor (1), *dep.*, accompany.

commisceō, -ēre, -uī, -xtum (-stum) (2), mix together.

commūnis, -e, common.

cōmō, -ere, -mpsī, -mptum (3), adorn (128).

compellō (1) accost, address.

complector, -ī, -xus (3), *dep.*, clasp, embrace.

complexus, -ūs, *m.*, embrace.

compōnō, -ere, -posuī, -positum (3), put together ; lay up (317) ; gather together (322) ; fit (486).

comprimō, -ere, -pressī, -pressum (3), press together ; check, allay (184).

concēdō, -ere, -cessī, -cessum (3), go away, withdraw ; subside (41).

concipiō, -ere, -cēpī, -ceptum, conceive.

concolor, -oris, of the same hue.

concurrō, -ere, -currī, -cursum (3), run together, clash.

concutiō, -ere, -cussī, -cussum, arouse (3), shake violently (237, 351).

condēnsus, -a, -um, packed together (497), dense, crowded.

conditor, -ōris, *m.*, founder.

condō, -ere, -didī, -ditum (3), found ; conceal (66).

conectō -ere -nexuī, -nexum (3), entwine, wreathe.

cōnfugiō, -ere, -fūgī, take refuge.

congredior, -ī, -gressus, *dep.*, meet.

coniungō, -ere, -iūnxī, -iūnctum (3), join together, unite.

coniūnx, -iugis, *c.*, husband, wife.

coniūrō (1), band together (5), conspire.

conlābor, -ī, -lāpsus (3), *dep.*, faint.

cōnscendō, -ere, -dī, -nsum (3), climb, ascend.

cōnscius, -a, -um, conscious.

cōnsessus, -ūs, *m.*, assembly.

cōnsistō, -ere, -stitī, -stitum (3), stand, halt (381) ; settle (10).

cōnsonō, -āre, -sonuī (1), resound.

cōnspectus, -a, -um, conspicuous.

cōnspiciō, -ere, -spēxī, -spectum, sight.

cōnsurgō, -ere, -surrēxī, -surrēctum (3), arise, rise up.

contemnō, -ere, -mpsī, -mptum (3), despise, scorn.

contemptor, -ōris, *m.*, despiser, scorner.

continuō, *adv.*, forthwith, straightway.

contrā, *adv.*, and *prep. with acc.*, opposite, against.

convellō, -ere, -vellī, -vulsum (3), tear up ; churn up (690).

cor, cordis, *n.*, heart.

cōram, *adv.*, and *prep. with acc.*, face to face, before.

corniger, -a, -um, horned.

cornū, -ūs, *n.*, horn.

corōna, -ae, *f.*, crown.

corpus, -oris, *n.*, body ; person (153) ; form (207).

corripiō, -ere, -ripuī, -reptum, seize.

coruscō (1), brandish.

coruscus, -a, -um, flashing.

crāstinus, -a, -um, to-morrow's.

creātrīx, -īcis, *f.*, mother.

crēdō, -ere, -didī, -ditum (3), believe (*often with dat.*).

crēscō, -ere, crēvī, crētum (3), increase, *intrans.*

Crēsius, -a, -um, Cretan.

crētus, -a, -um, sprung from (135) (*perf. part. pass. of* crēscō).

crīnis, -is, *m.*, hair.

crista, -ae, *f.*, crest, plume.

crūdēlis, -e, bloody, cruel.

cruentus, -a, -um, bloody.

cruor, -ōris, *m.*, blood, gore.

cubīle, -is, *n.*, bed, couch.

culmen, -inis, *n.*, roof, gable (456).

culmus, -ī, *m.*, thatch.

cultor, -ōris, *m.*, husbandman.

cultum, -ī, *n.*, tilled land.

cultus, -ūs, *m.*, culture ; civilisation (316).

cum, *conj.*, when.

cum, *prep. with abl.*, with.

cumulō (1), heap up.

cunctor (1), *dep.*, hesitate.

cūnctus, -a, -um, all.

cupidus, -a -um, eager, desirous.

cupiō, -ere, -īvī, -ītum, desire.

cūra, -ae, *f.*, care, anxiety.

Curēs, -ium, *m. pl.*, Cures (*capital of the Sabines*); =Sabines (638).

cūrō (1), care for : refresh (607).

curriculum, -ī, *n.*, course.

currō, -ere, cucurrī, cursum (3), run.

currus, -ūs, *m.*, chariot.

cursus, -ūs, *m.*, course ; *in abl.* =running.

custōdiō (4), guard, hold captive.

custōs, -ōdis, *c.*, guard, guardian.

Cyclades, -um, *f. pl.*, the Cyclades (*islands in Eastern Mediterranean*).

Cyclōps, -ōpis, *m.*, the Cyclops.

Cyllēnē, -ēs *or* ae, *f.*, Cyllene (*mountain in Arcadia*).

Cytherēa, -ae, *f.*, *a name of* Venus, *to whom the island of Cythera was sacred.*

Dahae, -ārum, *m. pl.*, the Dahae, a Scythian tribe.

Danaī, -ōrum *or* -um, *m. pl.*, the Danaans, the Greeks.

(daps), dapis, *f.*, feast, banquet.

Dardania, -ae, *f.*, Dardania (*a name of Troy*).

Dardanius, -a, -um, Trojan.

Dardanus, -ī, *m.*, Dardanus (*legendary king of Troy*).

Daunius, -a, -um, Daunian, Apulian *or* Rutulian.

dē, *prep. with abl.*, from ; down from.

dea, -ae, *f.*, goddess.

dēbeō (2), owe, ought.

dēbitus, -a, -um, owed, due.

decem, ten.

dēcolor, -ōris, degenerate (326).

decus, -oris, *n.*, glory, honour.

dēfendō, -ere, -ndī, -nsum (3) defend.

dēfīxus, -a, -um, (*perf. part. pass.*, *of* defigō, I fasten down), downcast.

dēfluō, -ere, -flūxī, -fluxum (3), float *or* flow down.

dehinc, *adv.*, then.

dehīscō (3), split open, gape.

dēiciō, -ere, -iēcī, -iectum, throw down ; rain upon (428).

deinde, *adv.*, thereafter, next.

dēligō, -ere, -lēgī, -lēctum (3), choose, select.

delphīn, -īnis, *m.*, dolphin.

dēlubrum, -ī, *n.*, shrine.

dēmittō, -ere, -mīsī, -mīssum (3), let down ; *in pass.*, hang down (460).

dēmō, -ere, dēmpsī, dēmptum (3), take away.

dēnī, -ae, -a, ten each.

dēns, dentis, *m.*, tooth.

dēprendō, -ere, -dī, -nsum (3), catch unawares.

dēscendō, -ere, -dī, -nsum (3), descend, go down.

dēsecō, -āre, -uī, -ctum (1), cut off, sever.

dēserō, -ere, -ruī, -rtum (3), abandon, desert.

dēsuper, *adv.*, from above.

dētegō, -ere, -tēxī, -tēctum (3), uncover, reveal.

dēterior, -ius, worse, inferior.

deus, -ī, *m.*, god.

dēvēxus, -a, -um, (*perf. part. pass.*, *of* devehō, I carry down), sloping (280).

dēvinciō, -īre, -nxī, -nctum (4), bind fast.

dexter, -tra, -trum, on the right.

dextra, -ae, *f.*, right hand.

dīcō, -ere, -xī, -ctum (3), say, tell.

dictum, -ī, *n.*, word ; saying.

dīdō, -ere, -didī, -ditum (3) spread abroad.

diēs, -ēī, *m.*, day.

differō, -ferre, distulī, dīlātum, put off, (173) ; tear asunder (643).

dīgnus, -a, -um, worthy ; fitting.

dīgressus, -ūs, *m.*, parting.

dīligō, -ere, -lēxī, -lēctum (3), love.

dīmittō, -ere, -mīsī, -mīssum (3), dismiss.

Diomēdēs, -is, *m.*, Diomede (*a Greek, and founder of Arpi in Apulia*).

Dīra, -ae, *f.*, (*lit.* dread one), a Fury.

dīrus, -a, -um, dire, dread.

Dīs, Dītis, *m.*, Dis (*god of the underworld*).

discēdō, -ere, -cessī, -cessum (3), depart.

discessus, -ūs, *m.*, departure.

discīnctus, -a, -um, ungirt.

discordia, -ae, *f.*, strife, discord ; (*also personified*),˙Discord.

dīsiciō, -ere, -iēcī, -iectum, dash to pieces (290) ; overthrow (355).

dīspergō, -ere, -sī, -sum (3), scatter, spread abroad.

dissultō (1), leap apart.

dīva, -ae, *f.*, goddess.

dīvellō, -ere, -vellī *or* vulsī, -vulsum (3), tear away.

dīversus, -a, -um, opposite.

dīvidō, -ere, -vīsī, -vīsum (3), divide.

dīvīnus, -a, -um, divine.

dīvus, -ī, *m.*, god.

dō, dare, dedī, datum (1), give ; poenās dare, to pay the penalty ; vēla dāre, to set sail.

doceō, -ēre, -uī, -ctum (2), teach, tell.

dolor, -ōris, *m.*, wrath (220) ; resentment (501).

dolus, -ī, *m.*, treachery, guile, trick.

domus, -ūs, *f.*, house, home.

dōnec, *conj.*, until.

dōnum, -ī, *n.*, gift.

dorsum, -ī, *n.*, back, ridge.

dubitō (1), hesitate.

dūcō, -ere, -xī, -ctum, lead ; prolong (55).

ductor, -ōris, *m.*, leader, guide.

dulcis, -e, sweet.

dum, *conj.*, while.

(dūmus, -ī), *m.*, *only in pl.*, thicket.

duo, -ae, -o, two.

duplicō (1), double.

dūrō (1), last, endure.

dūrus, -a, -um, hard, pitiless.

dux, ducis, *c.*, leader.

ē (=ex), *prep. with abl.*, out of, from : (*of time*) after.

ecce, *interj.*, lo! see!

edō, -ere (*or* ēsse), ēdī, ēsum (3), eat.

ēdō, -ere, -didī, -ditum (3), beget (137).

ēdoceō, -ēre, -uī, -ctum (2), inform ; announce (13).

ēdūcō, -ere, -xī, -ctum (3), bring up, rear.

efferō, -ferre, extulī, ēlātum, uplift, raise.

efferus, -a, -um, fierce, savage (484), frenzied (205).

effētus, -a, -um, exhausted, worn out.

effor (1), *dep.*, utter, speak forth.

effulgeō, -ēre (*also* -ere), -sī (2), gleam, be ablaze.

effultus, -a, -um, propped up.

effundō, -ere, -fūdī, -fūsum (3), pour forth.

ēgelidus, -a, -um, cold, cool.

egēnus, -a, -um, needy.

egeō (2), need (*with gen.*, 299).

ego, meī, *pers. pron.*, I.

ēgredior, -ī, -gressus, *dep.*, come *or* step forth, issue.

ēgregius, -a, -um, illustrious, distinguished.

ēiciō, -ere, -iēcī, -iectum, cast forth.

ēlābor, -ī, -lapsus (3), *dep.*, escape.

Ēlectra, -ae, *f.*, Electra (*a daughter of Atlas*).

ēlectrum, -ī, *n.*, electrum (*an alloy of gold and silver*).

ēlīdō, -ere, -sī, -sum (3), force *or* squeeze out : strangle (289).

ēmūniō (4), fortify, block (227).

ēn, *interj.*, lo! behold!

ēnārrābilis, -e, explainable ; nōn enarrabile = ineffable.

enim, *conj.*, for.

ēnitor, -ī, -nīxus *or* -nīsus (3), *dep.*, bring forth, bear (44).

ēnsis, -is, *m.*, sword.

eō, īre, iī (īvī), itum, go.

epulae, -ārum, *f. pl.*, feast, banquet.

eques, -itis, *m.*, horseman.

equidem, *adv.*, truly, indeed.

equitātus, -ūs, *m.*, cavalry.

equus, -ī, *m.*, horse.

ergō, *adv.*, therefore.

ērigō, -ere, -rēxī, -rēctum (3), raise up : *in pass.*, rise.

erīlis, -e, master's.

ēripiō, -ere, -puī, -eptum, snatch away, seize.

et, *conj.*, and ; *adv.*, too, also.

etenim, *conj.*, and indeed.

etiam, *adv.*, even, also.

Etrūria, -ae, *f.*, Etruria.

Etruscus, -a, -um, Etruscan.

Euphrātēs, -is, *m.*, the Euphrates.

Eurus, -ī, *m.*, the South-East Wind.

Eurystheus, -eī, *m.*, Eurystheus (*king of Mycenae*).

Evandrus, -ī, *m.*, Evander.

eventus, -ūs, *m.*, issue.

ēvinciō, -īre, -nxī, -nctum (4), bind.

ēvomō, -ere, -uī, -itum (3), belch forth.

exārdēscō, -ere, -ārsī, -ārsum (3), blaze forth.

excidium, -ī, *n.*, destruction.

excipiō, -ere, -cēpī, -ceptum, welcome (124).

excitō (1), rouse *or* stir up.

exedō, -ere, -ēdī, -ēsum (3), hollow out (418).

exeō, -īre, -iī (-īvī), -itum, go forth.

exerceō (2), employ, ply (378) ; keep at (412) ; work upon (424).

exhortor (1), *dep.*, encourage, exhort.

exiguus, -a, -um, mean, scanty.

exim, *adv.*, then, next.

eximō, -ere, -ēmī, -ēmptum (3), take away.

expediō, (4), solve, settle.

expellō, -ere, -pulī, -pulsum (3), drive away.

expleō, -ēre, -plēvī, -plētum (2), sate, glut.

exquīrō, -ere, -quīsīvī, -quīsītum (3), inquire into (312).

exsors, -tis, chosen.

exspectō (2), hope for, expect.

exstinguō, -ere, -nxī, -nctum (3), put out, extinguish ; slay.

exsul, -is, *c.*, exile.

exsultō (1), dance.
exta, -ōrum, *n. pl.,* meat.
extemplō, *adv.,* forthwith.
externus, -a, -um, foreign (503).
exterreō (2), dismay, affright.
extimēscō, -ere, -timuī (2), be afraid, dread.
extrēmus, -a, -um, remotest, farthest ; **extrēma,** *n. pl.,* ends (333).
extundō, -ere, -tudī, -tūsum (3), hammer out, emboss.
exuō, -ere, -uī, -ūtum (3), strip.

fabrīlis, -e, of the forge *or* smithy.
faciēs, -ēī, *f.,* appearance (194) ; face ; shape (298).
facilis, -e, easy.
faciō, -ere, fēcī, factum, make, do; *pass.,* **fiō, fierī, factus,** am made, become.
factum, -ī, *n.,* deed, action.
fallō, -ere, fefellī, falsum (3), deceive, cheat.
fāma, -ae, *f.,* repute, fame (132, 731) ; rumour (554).
famēs, -is, *f.,* hunger.
famula, -ae, *f.,* maid-servant.
famulus, -ī, *m.,* servant, slave.
fās, *n. indecl.,* divine law *or* right ; *used as a predic. adj.,* lawful, permitted.
fastīgium, -ī, *n.,* summit, roof.
fateor, -ērī, fassus (2), *dep.,* confess, own.
fātidicus, -a, -um, prophetic.
fātifer, -era, -erum, fateful, death-dealing.
fatīgō (1), tire, weary ; pass ceaselessly (94).
fātum, -ī, *n.,* fate, doom, destiny.
faucēs, -ium, *f pl.,* throat.

Faunus, -ī, *m.,* Faunus ; *in pl.,* the Fauns.
faveō, -ēre, fāvī, fautum (2), favour (*often with dat.*) : **faventēs,** graciously (173).
fel, fellis, *n.,* gall, bile.
fēmina -ae *f.,* woman.
feriō, -īre, (4 *defect.*), strike.
ferō, ferre, tulī, lātum, carry, bring, extol (288) ; lead (*intr.,* 212) ; **se ferre** (199), move ; *in pass.,* glide (549).
Ferōnia, -ae, *f.,* Feronia, *an ancient Italian goddess.*
ferrum, -ī, *n.,* iron, sword.
ferveō (2), glow *or* seethe with rage ; be stirring (677).
fervidus, -a, -um, hot, fiery.
fervō, -ere, *an old form of* **ferveo,** *above.*
fessus, -a, -um, weary, worn out.
fētus, -a, -um, with young ; newly delivered.
fētus, -ūs, *m.,* brood, litter.
fidēs, -eī, *f.,* trust ; pledge (*of friendship*), (150).
fīdūcia, -ae, *f.,* trust, confidence.
fīdus, -a, -um, trusty, faithful, loyal.
fīlia, -ae, *f.,* daughter.
fīlius, -ī, *m.,* son.
fingō, -ere, fīnxī, fīctum (3), make (365) ; shape (634) ; portray (726).
fīnis, -is, *m.,* end ; *in pl.,* territory (159).
fīnitimus, -a, -um, neighbouring.
fīō, *see* facio.
fīrmō (1), strengthen, confirm.
flagellum, -ī, *n.,* whip, scourge.
flamma, -ae, *f.,* flame, fire ; torch (283).

flectō, -ere, -xī, -xum (3), bend ;
soften (384).

fleō, -ēre, flēvī, flētum (2), weep,
weep for.

flexus, -ūs, *m.*, reach (*of a river*,
95).

flōreō (2), bloom, flourish.

flōs, flōris, *m.*, bloom (160) (*lit.*
flower).

fluctuō (1), waver.

fluctus, -ūs, *m.*, wave.

flūmen, -inis, *n.*, river.

fluō, -ere, -ūxī, -uxum (3), flow ;
drip (487).

fluvius, -ī, *m.*, river.

foedus, -eris, *n.*, treaty, alliance.

folium, -ī, *n.*, leaf.

follis, -is, *m.*, bellows.

fōns, fōntis, *m.*, spring, fountain.

(for), fārī (*dep., defect.*), speak, say.

forceps, -ipis, *f.*, tongs.

foris, -is, *f.*, door.

fōrma, -ae, *f.*, form, beauty.

fornāx, -ācis, *f.*, furnace.

fōrs, *abl.*, fōrte, *f.*, chance.

fortis, -e, brave, strong.

fōrtūna, -ae, *f.*, fortune, chance ;
also personified, the goddess
Fortune.

forum, -ī, *n.*, market-place, the
Forum.

foveō, -ēre, fōvī, fōtum (2), embrace, caress ; fondle (388).

fragor, -ōris, *m.*, roar ; clamour
(497).

fremō, -ere, -uī, -itum (3), mur-
mur.

frēnum, -ī, *n.*, bridle.

frētus, -a, -um, *with abl.*, relying
on.

frōndōsus, -a, -um, leafy.

frōns, -ndis, *f.*, leaf.

fruor, -ī, frūctūs (3) *dep., with abl.*,
enjoy.

fuga, -ae, *f.*, flight ; escape from
(251).

fugiō, -ere, fūgī, fugitum, flee.

fulciō, -īre, -sī, -tum (4), fasten,
secure.

fulgeō, -ēre, -sī (2), gleam.

fulgō, -ere, *an older form of* fulgeo.

fulgor, -ōris, *m.*, lightning : flash
of lightning.

fulmen, -inis, *n.*, thunderbolt.

fulvus, -a, -um, tawny.

fūmifer, -era, -erum, smoke-laden
(255).

fūmō (1), smoke.

fūmus, -ī, *m.*, smoke.

fundō (1), found, build.

fundō, -ere, fūdī, fūsum (3), bring
forth, bear (139) ; pour forth
(*words*, 584).

fūnis, -is, *m.*, rope ; sheet.

fūnus, -eris, *n.*, death ; (*lit.*
funeral).

fur, furis, *m.*, thief.

furia, -ae, *f.*, frenzy, anger : *personified* Furiae, the Furies
(669).

furō, -ere (3), rage, be furious.

fuscus, -a, -um, dark, dusky.

futūrum, -ī, *n.*, the future.

gaesum, -i, *n.*, javelin (*Gallic
weapon*).

galea, -ae, *f.*, helmet.

Gallus, -ī, *m.*, a Gaul.

gaudeō, -ēre, gavīsus (2), *semi-
dep.*, rejoice.

gelidus, -a, -um, cold ; cool (597).

Gelōnī, -ōrum, *m. pl.*, the Geloni
(*a Scythian tribe*).

gelū, -ūs, *n.*, cold.

geminus, -a, -um, *lit.* twin ; two.

gemitus, -ūs, *m.,* groan; sound.

gemō, -ere, -uī, -itum (3), sigh, groan.

gēna, -ae, *f.,* cheek.

generō (1), beget.

genetrīx, -īcis, *f.,* mother.

genitor, -ōris, *m.,* father.

gēns, gentis, *f.,* race, people.

genus, generis, *n.,* race, kind, generation (628).

gerō, -ere, gessī, gestum (3), carry on.

Gēryonēs, -ae, *m.,* Geryones (*a three-bodied giant*).

glaucus, -a, -um, grey.

glomerō (1), amass ; roll up (254).

Gorgō, -onis, *f.,* a Gorgon, Medusa.

gradior, -ī, gressūs, *dep.,* walk.

Grāiugena, -ae, *m.,* a Greek.

Grāius, -a, -um, Greek.

grāmineus, -a, -um, grassy.

grātus, -a, -um, pleasing.

gravis, -e, heavy ; stern.

gravō (1), make heavy.

gremium -ī, *n.,* lap.

gressus, -ūs, *m.,* step, walk.

grex, gregis, *m.,* (*lit.* flock), litter (85).

guttur, -uris, *n.,* throat.

habeō (2), have, hold.

habitō (1), inhabit.

habitus, -ūs, *m.,* style.

hāc, *adv.,* this way.

haereō, -ēre, haesī, haesum (2), cleave fast to.

harūndō, -inis, *f.,* reed.

harūspex, -icis, *m.,* soothsayer, seer.

hasta, -ae, *f.,* spear, lance.

haud, *adv.,* not.

Herculeus, -a, -um, of Hercules.

hērōs, -ōis, *m.,* hero.

Hēsionē, -ēs *or* **-ae,** *f.,* Hesione (*daughter of Laomedon*).

Hesperia, -ae, *f.,* Hesperia, *i.e.* the Western Land, Italy.

Hesperis, -idis, *f ,* Italian.

hesternus, -a, -um, yesterday's.

heu, *interj.,* alas!

hīc, haec, hōc, this.

hīc, *adv.,* here.

hinc, *adv.,* hence, from here ; **hinc, hinc,** on this side, on that.

hōc, *see* **hūc.**

homō, -inis, *m.,* man.

honōs, -ōris, *m.,* honour (617) ; worship ; sacrifice (76, 102, 189) ; service (268) ; tribute (339).

horrendus, -a -um, dreadful.

horreō, (2), be rough (654).

horridus, -a, -um, rough, bristling.

horrifer, -era, -erum, dread, terrible.

horrificus, -a, -um, frightful.

hospes, -itis, *c.,* guest (123, 346).

hostis, -is, *c.,* enemy.

hūc, *adv.,* hither, here.

humilis, -e, lowly.

humus, -ī, *f.,* earth, ground, soil.

Hylaeus, -ī, *m.,* Hylaeus (*a Centaur*).

iaceō (2), lie, lie down.

iaciō, -ere, iēcī, iactum, throw.

iactō (1), throw, hurl.

iam, *adv.,* now, already.

iamdūdum, *adv.,* now for long.

Iāniculum, -ī, *n.,* the Janiculum (*one of the seven hills of Rome*).

iānitor, -ōris, *m.,* door-keeper

Iānus, -ī, *m.*, Janus (*Italian god*).

Iāpyx, -ygis, *m.*, the Iapyx (*the West-North-West Wind*).

ibi, *adv.*, there, then.

ictus, -ūs, *m.*, blow.

īdem, eadem, idem, the same.

īgnārus, -a, -um, ignorant.

īgneus, -a, -um, fiery.

Īgnipotēns, -ntis, *m.*, Vulcan.

īgnōtus, -a, -um, unknown.

īlex, -icis, *f.*, holm-oak.

Īliacus, -a, -um, of Ilium (= Troy); Trojan.

īlicet, *adv.*, at once, forthwith.

ille, -a, -ud, that ; *also as pronoun*, he, she, it ; they.

illīc, *adv.*, there.

illūc, *adv.*, thither, there.

imāgō, -inis, *f.*, likeness ; image (23, 557) ; picture (730) ; semblance (671).

imber, -bris, *m.*, shower, squall.

immānis, -e, vast, huge, immense.

immittō, -ere, -mīsī, -mīssum (3), let in (246) ; slacken (708).

immortālis, -e, immortal.

impavidus, -a, -um, unafraid, dauntless.

impediō (4), hinder ; encircle (449).

impellō, -ere, -pulī, -pulsum (3), clash (3) ; thrust (239).

imperfectus, -a, -um, unfinished.

imperium, -ī, *n.*, command.

impleō, -ēre, -plēvī, -plētum (2), fill.

impōnō, -ere, -posuī, -positum (3), place upon.

imprōvīsō, *adv.*, unforeseen.

impulsus, -ūs, *m.*, shock.

īmus, -a, -um, lowest, bottom of.

in, *prep. with abl.*, in, on ; *with acc.*, into, on to.

inaccessus, -a, -um, inaccessible.

inārdēscō, -ere, -ārsī (3), glow.

inausus, -a, -um, undared.

incassum, *adv.*, in vain ; to no purpose.

incēdō, -ere, -cessī, -cessum (3), advance, move.

incendium, -ī, *n.*, fire.

incendō, -ere, -dī, -sum (3), burn, kindle ; set fire to (562).

incertus, -a, -um, uncertain, doubtful.

incipiō, -ere, -cēpī, -ceptum, begin.

inclūdō, -ere, -sī, -sum (3), shut in.

incolō, -ere, -coluī, -cultum (3), inhabit.

incolumis, -e, safe, unharmed.

incommodum, -ī, *n.*, misfortune.

incrēbrēscō, -ere, -crēbruī (3), grow, spread.

increpō, -āre, -uī, -itum (1), crash.

incumbō, -ere, -cubuī, -cubitum (3), lean on (108) ; fall to a task (444).

incūs, -ūdis, *f.*, anvil.

inde, *adv.*, then, thence.

indicium, -iī, *n.*, sign, trace, track.

indigena, -ae, *m.*, native.

indīgnor (1), *dep.*, chafe at.

indocilis, -e, unteachable.

indomitus, -a, -um, untamed.

indubitō (1), doubt ; mistrust (*with dat.*, 404).

indūcō, -ere, -xī, -ctum (3), clothe.

indulgeō, -ēre, -sī, -tum (2), be kind to ; grant to.

Indus -ī, *m.*, an Indian.

inēlūctābilīs, -e, inevitable

inexplētus, -a, -um, insatiate.

īnfandus, -a, -um, unspeakable ; impious (489).

īnfernus, -a, -um, infernal.

īnferō, -ferre, -tulī, -lātum, bring in.

īnfōrmis, -e, shapeless.

īnfōrmō (1), shape.

īnfrā, adv., and prep. with acc., below, beneath.

īnfrendō (3), gnash the teeth.

īnfundō, -ere, -fūdī, -fūsum (3), pour into ; in pass., sink into (406).

ingēns, -ntis, vast, huge, monstrous.

ingredior, -ī, -gressus, dep., enter ; move (309).

ingruō, -ere, -uī (3), rush upon ; threaten (535).

inhaereō, -ēre, -haesī, -haesum (2), cleave or cling fast to.

inimīcus, -a, -um, hostile.

inīquus, -a, -um, unjust, cruel.

innectō, -ere, -nexuī, -nexum (3), interweave (277) ; encircle (661).

innītor, -ī, -nīxus or -nīsus (3), dep., lean on.

innō (1), float upon (93) ; swim across (651).

inopīnus, -a, -um, unforeseen, unexpected.

inops, -is, poor, meagre, scant.

inquam, -is, -it, -iunt, defect. vb., say.

īnscius, -a, -um, unknowing, ignorant.

īnsequor, -ī, -sɛcūtus (3), dep., pursue ; harry (147).

īnsīdō, -ere, -sēdī, -sessum (3), settle.

īnsīgne, -is, n., sign ; ensign (506) ; device (683).

īnsīgnis, -e, conspicuous ; glorious, fine (166).

īnsonō, -āre, -uī, -itum (1), resound.

īnspērātus, -a, -um, unexpected, unforeseen.

īnspīrō (1), breathe into, inspire.

īnstaurō (1), renew (283).

īnstō, -āre, -stitī (1), threaten, press upon (sometimes with dat.).

īnstruō, -ere, -xī, -ctum (3), equip.

īnsuētus, -a, -um, unaccustomed.

īnsula, -ae, f., island.

īnsultō (1), trample upon.

īnsurgō, -ere, -surrēxī, -surrēctum (3), rise, rise up.

intendō, -ere, -dī, -ntum (3), stretch.

inter, prep. with acc., between, among.

intereā, adv., meanwhile.

intertextus, -a -um, interwoven.

intonō, -āre, -uī, -itum (1), thunder.

intrā, adv., and prep. with acc., within.

intractātus, -a, -um, untried.

intrō (1), enter.

invehō, -ere, -xī, -ctum (3), carry in.

inveniō, -īre, -vēnī, -ventum (4), come upon ; find.

invīctus, -a, -um, unconquered.

invideō, -ēre, -vīdī, -vīsum (2), begrudge.

invīsō, -ere, -sī, -sum (3), visit.

invīsus, -a, -um, hateful.

invītō (1), entertain (178).

involvō, -ere, -vī, -ūtum (3), enfold ; envelop (253).

Iovem, Iovis, *see* Iuppiter.

ipse, -a, -um, -self, he himself, *etc.* very.

īra, -ae, *f.*, anger, wrath, passion.

is, ea, id, that : *also as pronoun*, he, she, it, they.

ita, *adv.*, so, thus.

Italus, -a, -um, Italian : *also as noun*, an Italian (678).

iter, itineris, *n.*, journey, voyage.

iterum, *adv.*, again, a second time.

iubeō, -ēre, iussī, iūssum (2), bid.

iugum, -ī, *n.*, yoke ; ridge (480).

iungō, -ere, -nxī, -nctum (3), join (467) ; make (*a treaty*, 56) ; yoke (316).

Iūnō, -ōnis, *f.*, Juno (*wife of Jupiter*).

Iuppiter, Iovis, *m.*, Jupiter, Jove.

iustus, -a, -um, righteous, just.

iuvenālis, -e, youthful.

iuvenca, -ae, *f.*, heifer.

iuvencus, -ī, *m.*, steer.

iuvenis, -is, *m.*, young man, warrior (105, 112).

iuventās, -tātis, *f.*, youth.

iuventūs, -tūtis, *f.*, youth ; warriors (499, 606).

iuvō, -āre, iūvī, iūtum (1), help, aid.

iūxtā, *adv.*, near (416), by his side (308) ; *as prep. with acc.*, near.

labefaciō, -ere, -fēcī, -factum, make to totter ; *in perf. partic. pass.*, yielding, melting.

lābor, -ī, lapsus (3), *dep.*, glide ; fall (664).

labor, -ōris, *m.*, work, labour, toil ; trouble.

labōrō (1), work at *or* upon.

lābrum, -ī, *n.*, basin.

lacertus, -ī, *m.*, arm.

lacrima, -ae, *f.*, tear.

lacrimō (1), weep.

lacteus, -a, -um, milk-white.

lacus, -ūs, *m.*, pool ; tank, cistern (451).

laetitia, -ae, *f.*, joy.

laetus, -a, -um, joyful, happy, merry.

laeva, -ae, *f.*, the left hand.

laevus, -a, -um, left ; on the left side *or* hand.

lambō, -ere (3), lick.

lāniger, -era, -erum, bearing wool.

lanx, lancis, *f.*, dish, platter.

Lāomedontiadēs, -ae, *m.*, son of Laomedon.

Lāomedontius, -a, -um, Trojan (*Laomedon was father of Priam*).

laqueāria, -ium, *n. pl.*, panelled ceiling.

lār, laris, *m.*, a household god.

lātē, *adv.*, far and wide.

latebrōsus, -a, -um, full of hiding-places, sheltered.

lateō (2), lie hid.

Latīnus, -ī, *m.*, Latinus (*king of the Laurentians*).

Latīnus, -a, -um, of Latium, Latin.

Latium, -ī, *n.*, Latium.

lātrātor, -ōris, *m.*, a barking dog.

latus, -eris, *n.*, side (459) ; coast.

lātus, -a, -um, wide, broad.

Laurēns, -ntis, Laurentian, of Laurentum ; *also as noun*, a Laurentian.

Laurentum, -ī, *n.*, Laurentum (*capital of Latium*).

laus, laudis, *f.*, praise ; praise-worthy deed (273) ; *in pl.*, glories (287).

lautus, -a, -um, splendid, sumptu-ous ; stately, brilliant (361).

laxus, -a, -um, slackened, loose.

lēgātus, -ī, *m.*, envoy.

legiō, -ōnis, *f.*, host.

legō, -ere, lēgī, lēctum (3), choose.

Leleges, -um, *m. pl.*, the Leleges.

Lemnius, -a, -um, of Lemnos (*island in the Aegean Sea*).

lēniō (4), calm.

leō, -ōnis, *m.*, lion.

Lernaeus, -a, -um, of Lerna.

lētum, -ī, *n.*, death.

Leucātē, -ēs, *m.*, Leucate.

lēvis, -e, smooth.

levō (1), relieve.

lēx, lēgis, *f.*, law.

libēns, -ntis, willing:

lībertās, -tātis, *f.*, freedom, liberty.

lībō (1), pour libation.

Libystis, -idis, *f.*, Libyan, African.

licet (2), *impers.*, it is allowed : licitus, *perf. partic. pass.*, un-trammelled, free (468).

līmen, -inis, *n.*, threshold.

lingua, -ae, *f.*, tongue.

Liparē, *acc.* -en, *f.*, Lipara (*largest of the Aeolian Islands, north of Sicily*).

liquēscō (3), melt.

liquidus, -a, -um, molten.

lītoreus, -a, -um, of *or* on the shore.

lītus, -oris, *n.*, sea-shore.

locō (1), place, set.

locus, -ī, *m.*, *pl.* locī *or in neut. form,* loca, place, site.

longaevus, -a, -um, aged.

longē, *adv.*, far off, at a distance.

longus, -a, -um, long ; lingering (488).

loquor, -ī, locūtus (3), *dep.*, speak.

lōrīca, -ae, *f.*, corselet, breast-plate.

lūceō, -ēre, lūxī (2), glitter.

Lūcifer, -erī, *m.*, Lucifer, the morning star.

lūctāmen, -inis, *n.*, struggle, toil.

lūcus, -ī, *m.*, grove.

lūdō, -ere, -sī, -sum (3), play.

lūdus, -ī, *m.*, game.

lūmen, -inis, *n.*, light ; beam (69); eye (153).

lūna, -ae, *f.*, moon.

lupa, -ae, *f.*, she-wolf.

Lupercal, -ālis, *n.*, the Lupercal.

Lupercī, -ōrum, *m. pl.*, priests of Lupercus.

lūstrālis, -e, of purification.

lūstrō (1), scan.

lūx, lūcis, *f.*, light, day, dawn.

Lycaeus, -a, -um, Lycaean.

Lycius, -a, -um, of Lycia (*district in Asia Minor*).

Lydius, -a, -um, of Lydia (*dis-trict in Asia Minor*).

mactō (1), sacrifice ; slaughter (294).

Maeonia, -ae, *f.*, Maeonia (= Lydia).

Maeonius, -a, -um, Maeonian, Lydian.

maereō (2), mourn, grieve.

magister, -trī, *m.*, master.

magistra, -ae, *f.*, mistress ; in 442 *as adj.*, =sovereign.

māgnus, -a, -um, great, mighty.

Māia, -ae, *f.*, Maia (*daughter of Atlas, and mother of Mercury*).

māior, -us, *compar. of* māgnus.

mālō, mālle, māluī, prefer.

mandō (1), entrust.

maneō, -ēre, mānsī (2), remain.

mānēs, -ium, *m. pl.,* the Manes (*spirits of the dead*) ; ghosts ; the underworld (246).

manifestus, -a, -um, plain, clear.

Mānlius, -ī, *m.,* Marcus Manlius (*surnamed* Capitolinus).

manus, -ūs, *f.,* hand ; band (329).

mare, -is, *n.,* sea.

Mārs, Mārtis, *m.,* Mars (*the Roman god of war*) ; =war (495).

massa, -ae, *f.,* mass.

māter, -tris, *f.,* mother : matron (718).

mātūtīnus, -a, -um, early ; of *or* in the morning.

Māvors, -tis, *m.,* =Mars.

māximus, -a, -um, *superlative of* māgnus.

medius, -a, -um, middle of, mid.

medulla, -ae, *f.,* marrow.

membrum, -ī, *n.,* limb.

meminī, -isse, *defect. vb.,* remember.

memor, -oris, mindful.

memorō (1), speak of, tell.

mendāx, -ācis, lying, treacherous.

mēns, mentis, *f.,* mind ; purpose (400).

mēnsa, -ae, *f.,* table ; repast (283) ; *in pl.,* board (174).

Mercurius, -ī, *m.,* Mercury.

mereor (2), *dep.,* deserve, earn.

meritus, -a, -um, due ; justly due (189) ; righteous (501).

Messāpus, -ī, *m.,* Messapus (*Etruscan king*).

mēta, -ae, *f., lit.* turning point ; goal.

metallum, -ī, *n.,* metal, ore.

metus, -ūs, *m.,* fear.

Mettus, -ī, *m.,* Mettus Fufetius (*king of Alba*).

meus, -a, -um, my, mine.

Mezentius, -ī, *m.,* Mezentius (*king of Caere*).

micō, -āre, -uī (1), flicker, flash.

mīlitia, -ae, *f.,* warfare.

mīlle, thousand ; mīlia, -ium, *n. pl.,* thousands.

mina, -ae, *f.,* threat.

mināx, -ācis, threatening, menacing.

Minerva, -ae, *f.,* Minerva.

ministrō (1), serve.

minor (1), *dep.,* threaten.

minor, -ōris, *compar. of* parvus ; *in pl.,* minōrēs, posterity.

minus, *compar. adv.,* less.

mīrābilis, -e, wonderful.

mīror (1), *dep.,* marvel, wonder at.

misceō, -ēre, -uī, mīxtum *or* mīstum (2), mix, mingle.

miser, -era, -erum, hapless, wretched.

miserēscō, -ere, (3) pity (*with gen.,* 573).

miseror (1), *dep.,* pity.

mītis, -e, mild, gentle.

mittō, -ere, mīsī, mīssum (3), send.

moenia, -ium, *n. pl.,* walls (*of city*)

molāris, -is, *m.,* mill-stone.

mōlēs, -is, *f.,* mass, bulk.

mollis, -e, soft, tender ; cushioned (666).

monitum, -ī, *n.,* warning, advice.

mōns, montis, *m.,* hill, mountain.

mōnstrō (1), show, point out.

mōnstrum, -ī, *n.,* portent ; monster ; monstrous form (698).

monumentum, -ī, *n.*, record (312); memorial (356).

mora, -ae, *f.*, delay, hindrance.

Morinī, -ōrūm, *m. pl.*, the Morini.

morior, -ī, mortuus, *dep.*, die.

mors, mortis, *f.*, death.

mortuus, -a, -um, dead.

mōs, mōris, *m.*, custom; fixed manner of life (316); dē mōre, according to custom.

moveō, -ēre, mōvī, mōtum (2), move.

mox, *adv.*, soon.

mūgiō (4), bellow; peal (526).

mulceō, -ēre, -sī, -sum (2), fondle, caress.

Mulciber, -eris, *or* -erī, *m.*, Mulciber (*a name of Vulcan*).

multus, -a, -um, much, many.

mūrus, -ī, *m.*, wall.

mūnus, -eris, *n.*, honour (273); aid (464); name (519); gift (613).

nam, *conj.*, for.

namque, *conj.*, for, for indeed.

nāscor, -ī, nātus (3), *dep.*, am born.

nātus, -a, -um, *perf. part. of* nāscor, born of (59, 315).

nātus, -ī, *m.*, son, child, offspring.

nāvālis, -e, naval.

nāvis, -is, *f.*, ship.

nē, *adv.*, not; *conj.*, lest.

nebula, -ae, *f.*, cloud, mist; pall (258).

nec, *conj.*, and not, nor; nec . . . nec, neither . . . nor.

necdum, *adv.*, *and conj.*, and not yet, nor yet.

nec nōn, *adv.*, also, too.

necō (1), kill, slay .

nefās, *n.*, *indecl.*, impiety, crime; *as adj.*, impious.

negō (1), say . . . not, deny.

Nemea, -ae, *f.*, Nemea (*a city in Greece*).

Nemeus, -a, -um, of Nemea.

nemus, -oris, *n.*, grove, wood, forest.

nepōs, -ōtis, *m.*, *lit.* grandson; descendant.

Neptūnius, -a, -um, of Neptune.

Neptūnus, -ī, *m.*, Neptune (*god of the sea*).

neque, *see* nec.

nequeō, -īre, -īvī (4), *defect. vb.*, am unable.

nēquīquam, *adv.*, in vain.

Nēreus, -eī, *m.*, Nereus (*a god of the sea*).

neu *or* nēve, *adv.*, and not, nor.

nex, necis, *f.*, slaughter.

nī, *conj.*, unless.

nīdus, -ī, *m.*, nest.

niger, -gra, -grum, black.

nigrāns, -ntis, black.

nihil, *n.*, *indecl.*, nothing.

Nīlus, -ī, *m.*, the Nile.

nimbus, -ī, *m.*, thunder *or* storm cloud.

nisi, *conj.*, unless, except.

nītor, -ī, -xus *or* -sus (3), *dep.*, lean upon.

niveus, -a, -um, snowy; snow-white (720).

nōbilis, -e, famous, renowned, noble.

nōdus, -ī, *m.*, knot.

Nomades, -um, *m. pl.*, the Numidians (*pastoral people of Africa*).

nōmen, -inis, *n.*, name; fame (14)

nōn, *adv.*, not.

nōs, *plural of* ego, we, us.

nōscō, -ere, nōvi, nōtum (3), get to know ; *in perf.*, know.
noster, -tra, -trum, our.
nōtus, -a, -um, known.
noverca, -ae, *f.*, step-mother.
novō (1), renew.
novus, -a, -um, new.
nox, noctis, *f.*, night.
nūbēs, -is, *f.*, cloud.
nūbigena, -ae, cloud-born.
nūdus, -a, -um, naked.
nūllus, -a, -um, no ; *as pronoun,* none.
nūmen, -inis, *n.*, deity, divinity, divine will ; divine presence (186).
numerus, -ī, *m.*, number.
numquam, *adv.*, never.
nunc, *adv.*, now.
nūntius, -ī, *m.*, messenger : *as adj.*, with tidings.
nympha, -ae, *f.*, nymph.

ob, *prep. with acc.*, on account of.
obeō, -īre, -iī (iv.), -itum, cover (553).
ōbex, -icis, *m., and f.*, barrier, obstacle.
obiciō, -ere, -iēcī, -iectum, endanger, risk (145).
obsidiō, -iōnis, *f.*, siege.
obsitus, -a, -um, weighed down.
obstipēscō, -ere, -stipuī, (3), be astounded *or* amazed.
obtruncō (1), cut to pieces, butcher.
obvius, -a, -um, in the way (of) ; to meet.
occultō (1), hide.
Ōceanus, -ī, *m.*, Ocean (*god of the sea*) ; the Ocean (589).
ōcior, -ius, swifter.

ocrea, -ae, *f.*, greave.
oculus, -ī, *m.*, eye.
Oechalia, -ae, *f.*, Oechalia (*a city in Euboea, Greece*).
offerō, -ferre, obtulī, oblātum, offer ; offer to view (611).
ōlim, *adv.*, at times (391) ; formerly.
olīva, -ae, *f.*, olive.
Olympus, -ī, *m.*, Olympus (*in northern Greece, said to be the home of the gods*).
omnigenus, -a, -um, of all kinds.
omnipotēns, -entis, almighty.
omnis, -e, all, every.
onerō (1), burden ; onerātus, -a, -um, laden (284).
opācus, -a, -um, shady, dark.
oppidum, -ī, *n.*, town.
opportūnus, -a, -um, convenient, fit, suitable.
(ops), opis, *f.*, help ; aid (377) *in pl.*, resources, stores (171, 317) ; wealth (364).
optimus, -a, -um, *superl. of* bonus, best, noblest.
optō (1), desire (200, 405) ; choose (503).
opulentus, -a, -um, wealthy, powerful.
opus, -eris, *n.*, work.
ōra, -ae, *f.*, coast, country.
ōrāculum, -ī, *n.*, oracle.
ōrātor, -ōris, *m.*, envoy.
orbis, -is, *m.*, circle ; arch (97) ; sphere (137).
Orcus, -ī, *m.*, Orcus (=*Dis or Pluto, King of the underworld*).
ordo, -inis, *m.*, order ; array (722).
oriēns, -ntis, *m.*, the rising (sun), the East.
orior, -īrī, ortus (4), *dep.*, rise

ōrō (1), beg, pray.
ōs, ōris, *n.*, face.
os, ossis, *n.*, bone ; *in pl.*, frame (390).
ostendō, -ere, -dī, -ntum, (-nsum) (3), display.
ōstium, -ī, *n.*, entrance.

pācifer, -era, -erum, peaceful.
palla, -ae, *f.*, robe.
Pallantēum, -ī, *n.*, Pallanteum (*town on site of later Rome*).
Pallas, -adis, *f.*, Pallas Athena (=Minerva).
Pallas, -ntis, *acc.*, Pallanta, *m.*, Pallas, (1) *great-grandfather of Evander* ; (2) *son of Evander*.
palleō (2), turn pale.
pallidus, -a, -um, pale, pallid.
palma, -ae, *f.*, palm (*of hand*).
palūs, -ūdis, *f.*, marsh, mere.
Pān, -os, *acc.* -a, *m.*, Pan (*god of woods and shepherds*).
pandō, -ere, -dī, passum *or* pānsum (3), spread out, lay open ; open (712).
pangō, -ere, pepigī, pāctum (3), determine upon.
panthēra, -ae, *f.*, panther.
parcō, -ere, pepercī, parsum (3), *with dat.*, spare, husband.
parēns, -ntis, *m*, *or f.*, parent, father, mother.
pariō, -ere, peperī, partum, gain, win (317).
pariter, *adv.*, likewise.
parō (1), prepare.
Parrhasius, -a, -um, Parrhasian, =Arcadian.
pars, partis, *f.*, part ; direction.
parvus, -a, -um, small.
passim, *adv.*, everywhere.

pateō (2), be open *or* lie open.
pater, patris, *m.*, father.
patera, -ae, *f.*, dish, bowl.
paternus, -a, -um, father's.
patior, -ī, passus, *dep.*, suffer, bear.
patria, -ae, *f.*, native land.
patrius, -a, -um, father's ; ancestral.
paucī, -ae, -a, few.
paulātim, *adv.*, gradually.
pauper, -eris, humble (105, 360).
pavidus, -a, -um, fearful, trembling.
pāx, pācis, *f.*, peace.
pectus, -oris, *n.*, breast, heart.
pecus, -oris, *n.*, flock.
pecus, -udis, *f.*, beast ; *in pl.*, cattle.
pelagus, -ī, *n.*, sea, open sea.
Pelasgī, -ōrum, *m. pl.*, the Pelasgians.
pellis, -is, *f.*, skin, hide, pelt.
pellō, -ere, pepulī, pulsum (3), drive ; drive off *or* away (147).
penātēs, -ium, *m. pl.*, the Penates, household gods ; home (139).
pendeō, -ēre, pependī (2), hang.
penitus, *adv.*, deep within (242) ; utterly, entirely.
pēnsum, -ī, *n.*, task.
per, *prep. with acc.*, through, over.
percurrō, -ere, -currī, -cursum (3), run through.
percutiō, -ere, -cussī, -cussum, smite, kill.
perferō, -ferre, -tulī, -lātum, endure.
perficiō, -ere, -fēcī, -fectum, complete.
perfundō, -ere, -fūdī, -fūsum (3), pour over ; perfūsus (589), drenched, bathed.

Pergama, -ōrum, *n. pl.,* Pergama (*i.e. the citadel of Troy*).

perhibeō (2), say.

perīculum, -ī, *n.,* danger.

perpetuus, -a, -um, endless, enduring.

persolvō, -ere, -vī, -solūtum (3), pay in full, discharge; offer (62).

pervolitō, (1), fly through; flit about.

pēs, pedis, *m.,* foot.

petō, -ere, -īvī, -ītum (3), seek; make for.

pharetra, -ae, *f.,* quiver.

Pheneus, -eī, *m.,* Pheneus (*a town in Arcadia, Greece*).

Phoebus, -ī, *m.,* Phoebus, Apollo.

Pholus, -ī, *m.,* Pholus (*a Centaur*).

pīlentum, -ī, *n.,* carriage.

Pinarius, -a, -um, of the Pinarii.

pingō, -ere, pīnxī, pīctum (3), emblazon (588).

pinguis, -e, rich, fertile.

pius, -a, -um, dutiful, good.

placidus, -a, -um, calm, peaceful.

planta, -ae, *f.,* sole (*of the foot*).

plausus, -ūs, *m.,* applause.

plēnus, -a, -um, full.

plūrimus, -a, -um, *superl.,* of **multus,** very much, very many.

plūs, plūris, *compar.,* more; *in pl.,* more, many.

pōculum, -ī, *n.,* cup.

poena, -ae, *f.,* punishment, retribution; price (538).

poliō (4), polish, burnish.

pōnō, -ere, posuī, positum (3), place, set; put aside (329); lay aside (639); build (53).

pōns, pontis, *m.,* bridge.

pōpuleus, -a, -um, of the poplar-tree.

populus, -ī, *m.,* people.

pōpulus, -ī, *f.,* poplar.

porca, -ae, *f.,* sow.

porrigō, or **porgo, -ere, -rēxī, -rēctum** (3), reach out.

Porsenna, -ae, *m.,* (Lars) Porsenna (*king of Etruria*).

porta, -ae, *f.,* gate.

portentum, -ī, *n.,* portent, omen.

porticus, -ūs, *f.,* colonnade.

poscō, -ere, poposcī (3), demand; summon (477); challenge (614).

possum, posse, potuī, am able.

post, *adv., and prep. with acc.,* after; afterwards.

postis, -is, *m.,* door-post.

postquam, *conj.,* when, after.

Potitiī, -iōrum, *m. pl.,* the Potitii.

potentia, -ae, *f.,* power.

prae, *adv., and prep. with abl.,* before, in front of.

praecēdō, -ere, -cessī, -cessum (3) precede, go in front of.

praeceps, -itis, headlong.

praecīdō, -ere, -cīdī, -cīsum (3), cut sheer away (233).

praecipitō (1), cast off (443).

praecipuus, -a, -um, in the first place; before all.

praeclārus, -a, -um, brilliant, splendid, illustrious.

praefulgeō, -ēre (2), gleam, bright.

Praeneste, -is, *f.,* Praeneste (*town in Latium*).

praesēns, -ntis, instant.

praestāns, -ntis, surpassing.

praetendō, -ere, -tendī, -tēnsum (3), hold out.

praeter, *prep. with acc.,* beside, beyond, except.

praetereā, *adv.,* besides, moreover, in addition.

praeteritus, -a, -um, bygone, past.

precor (1), *dep.*, pray.

(prex), precem, prece, *acc. and abl. only, f.,* prayer, entreaty.

premō, -ere, pressī, pressum (3), press hard, attack.

Priamus, -ī, *m.,* Priam (*king of Troy*).

prīmum, *adv.,* first, at first.

prīmus, -a, -um, first.

prior, prius, former, earlier; first (469).

prīscus, -a, -um, olden, ancient.

prō, *prep. with abl.,* on behalf of, for.

proavus, -ī, *m.,* great-grandfather.

procerēs, -um, *m. pl.,* chiefs, chieftains.

procul, *adv.,* afar off, at a *or* in the distance.

procumbō, -ere, -cubuī, -cubitum (3), lie down.

prōdigium, -ī, *n.,* prodigy, portent; monster (295).

proelium, -ī, *n.,* battle.

profectō, *adv.,* certainly, indeed.

proficīscor, -ī, -fectus (3), *dep.,* set out, start.

profugus, -a, -um, exiled.

prōgredior, -ī, -gressus, *dep.,* go forward, advance.

prōlēs, -is, *f.,* offspring.

prōmissum, -ī, *n.,* promise.

prōmittō, -ere, -mīsī, -missum (3), promise.

prōnus, -a, -um, leaning forward; flowing downward (548).

prope, *adv., and prep., with acc.,* near.

propior, -ius, nearer.

propius, *compar. adv.,* more surely (78); nearer (556).

properō (1), hasten; speed (454).

propinquō (1), approach.

prōra, -ae, *f.,* prow, bows.

prōspectus, -ūs, *m.,* view.

prōtegō, -ere, -tēxī, -tēctum (3), protect.

prōtinus, *adv.,* forthwith.

prōtrahō, -ere, -trāxī, -tractum (3), drag out.

proximus, -a, -um, nearest, next.

pūbēs, -is, *f.,* youth.

puer, -erī, *m.,* boy.

pūgna, -ae, *f.,* fight, fighting, combat.

pūgnō (1), fight.

pulcher, -chra, -chrum, beautiful.

pulvereus, -a, -um, of dust.

puppis, -is, *f.,* stern, poop; =ship (497).

puter, -tris, -tre, crumbling.

putō (1), think.

Pyracmōn, -onis, *m.,* Pyracmon = ' Fire Anvil ' (*name of a Cyclops*).

quā, *adv.,* where.

quadrīgae, -ārum, *f. pl.,* four-horsed chariot.

quadripedāns, -ntis, galloping.

quaerō, -ere, -sīvī, -sītum (3), seek, ask.

quaesō (-ere), *only 1st prs. sg. and pl., pres. indic. act.,* pray, beseech.

quālis, -e, (1) *interrog.,* of what kind; (2) *relative* (of such a kind) as.

quam, *adv.,* than.

quamvis, *conj.,* although.

quandō, *conj.,* since.

quantum, *adv.,* as much as.

quantus, -a, -um, (1) *interrog.*, how great, (2) *relative*, as ; *with ellipsis of* tantus, as great as, as much as.

quārē, *adv., and conj.*, wherefore.

quatiō, -ere, —, quassum, shake.

quattuor, four.

-que, and ; -que . . . -que, both . . . and.

quercus, -ūs, *f.*, oak.

querēla, -ae, *f.*, plaint (215).

quī, quae, quod, *relat. pron.*, who, which, that ; what.

quī, quae, quod, *interrog. adj.*, which? what?

quia, *conj.*, because.

quīcumque, quae-, quod-, *rel. pron.*, whosoever, whatever.

quid, *adv.*, why?

quidem, *adv.*, indeed.

quiēs, -ētis, *f.*, rest, sleep.

quīn, *conj., with indic.*, why not? nay (485) ; *with subj.*, but that.

quīn etiam, *conj.*, nay more.

quis, quid, *interrog. pron.*, who? which? what?

quis, quid, *indefin. pron.*, any, anyone, anything, one.

quisquam, quaequam, quic- *or* quidquam (*only in negative or virtually negative sentences*), anyone, anything ; *neut.* quicquam, at all (140).

quisque, quaeque, quidque (*adj.* quodque), *indef. pron.*, each.

quisquis, *neut.* quidquid (*adj.*, quodquod), *rel. pron.*, whoever, whatever.

quīvīs, quaevīs, quidvīs (*adj.* quodvīs), *indef. pron.*, any (*you like*).

quō, *adv.*, whither, where to.

quod, *conj.*, because.

quondam, *adv.*, formerly ; at times.

quoniam, *conj.*, since.

quoque, *adv.*, also, too.

rabiēs, -ēī, *f.*, madness, fury.

radiāns, -ntis, beaming, shining.

radius, -ī, *m.*, ray of light (195, 623) ; shaft (*of rain*) (429).

rādīx, -īcis, *f.*, root.

rāmus, -ī, *m.*, branch.

rapidus, -a, -um, swift (442).

rapīna, -ae, *f.*, rapine, plunder.

rapiō, -ere, rapuī, raptum, snatch, seize, hasten ; hurry (21).

raptō (1), drag.

rārus, -a, -um, few ; straggling (98).

ratiō, -iōnis, *f.*, manner (49) ; reason (299).

ratis, -is, *f.*, ship.

raucus, -a, -um, hoarse.

recēns, -ntis, fresh.

recessus, -ūs, *m.*, lurking-place.

reclūdō, -ere, -sī, -sum (3), open.

recōgnōscō, -ere, -ōvī, -itum (3), review (721).

recoquō, -ere, -cōxī, -coctum (3), refine.

recordor (1), *dep.*, recall.

rēctor, -ōris, *m.*, ruler.

rēctus, -a, -um, straight.

recubō (1), lie *or* lie down.

reddō, -ere, -didī, -ditum (3), give back : return (217) ; se reddere, to return, *intrans.* (170).

redeō, -īre, -iī (-īvī), -itum, return, circle (47).

redūcō, -ere, -xī, -ctum (3), lead back.

reductus, -a, -um, remote, retired.

referō, -ferre, rettulī, relātum, bring back 560) ; return (*in answer*) (154).

reflectō, -ere, -xī, -xum (3), bend back.

refluō, -ere, -xī, -xum (3), ebb ; recoil (240).

refulgeō, -ēre, -sī (2), reflect, glitter.

rēgia, -ae, *f.*, (*royal*) palace.

rēgīna, -ae, *f.*, queen.

regiō, -ōnis, *f.*, quarter, region.

rēgnātor, -ōris, *m.*, ruler.

rēgnum, -ī, *n.*, kingdom, realm.

regō, -ere, -xī, -ctum (3), rule, guide.

religiō, -ōnis, *f.*, reverence (349) ; awe (598).

relinquō, -ere, -līquī, -līctum (3), leave.

reliquiae, -ārum, *f. pl.*, remains.

rēmigium, -ī, *n.*, rowers (80) ; rowing (94).

rēmus, -ī, *m.*, oar.

repentē, *adv.*, suddenly.

repercussus, -a, -um, reflected, mirrored.

repōnō, -ere, -posuī, -positum (3), restore.

reposcō, -ere, (3), demand back.

requiēs, -ētis, *f.*, rest, repose, respite.

rēs, reī, *f.*, a thing ; res divinae (306), a sacrifice.

reserō (1), unlock, unfasten.

reservō (1), store up ; keep (575).

resīdō, -ere, -sēdī, (3), sit *or* settle down.

resolvō, -ere, -solvī, -solūtum (3), dispel.

respiciō, -ere, -spēxī, -spectum, look back at.

resultō (1), *lit.* leap back ; re-echo (305).

retineō, -ēre, -tinuī, -tentum (2), hold back *or* in check.

retorqueō, -ēre, -rsī, -rtum (2), twist *or* fling back (460).

revehō, -ere, -vēxī, -vēctum (3), carry *or* bring back.

revellō, -ere, -vellī, -vulsum (3), tear off (262) ; tear up (691).

revīsō, -ere, -vīsī, -vīsum (3), revisit.

rēx, rēgis, *m.*, king ; prince (374).

Rhēnus, -ī, *m.*, the Rhine.

rigeō (2), am stiff.

rīma, -ae, *f.*, crack, chink.

rīpa, -ae, *f.*, (*river*) bank.

rīte, *adv.*, duly.

rīvus, -ī, *m.*, stream.

rōbur, -oris, *n.*, oak (315) ; cudgel (221) ; strength, flower (518).

rogō (1), ask.

Rōma, -ae, *f.*, Rome.

Rōmānus, -a, -um, Roman.

Rōmuleus, -a, -um, of Romulus.

Rōmulidae, -ārum, *m. pl.*, sons of Romulus.

Rōmulus, -ī, *m.*, Romulus.

rōrō (1), bedew ; *intrans.*, drip (645).

rōstrātus, -a, -um, beaked.

rōstrum, -ī, *n.*, beak, ram.

rota, -ae, *f.*, wheel.

ruber, -bra, -brum, red.

rubēscō, -ere (3), redden (*intrans.*).

rudō, -ere (3), roar.

ruīna, -ae, *f.*, downfall, destruction, ruin.

rūmor, -ōris, *m.*, cheers (90).

rumpō, -ere, rūpī, ruptum (3), break (225) ; burst ; break off (540).

ruō, -ere, ruī, rutum (3), fall (369); reel (525); rush (648, 689).

rūpēs, -is, *f.*, rock, crag.

rūrsus, *adv.*, again.

rutilō (1), glow, glow red.

rutilus, -a, -um, red.

Rutulī, -ōrum, *m. pl.*, the Rutulians (*tribe in Latium*).

Sabaeī, -ōrum, *m. pl.*, the Sabaeans (*people in Arabia*).

Sabellus, -a, -um, Sabine.

Sabīnus, -a, -um, Sabine.

sacer, -cra, -crum, sacred; *as neut. noun*, ceremony (111); rite (172, 270, 302).

sacerdōs, -ōtis, *c.*, priest, priestess.

sacrō (1), consecrate.

saec(u)lum, -ī, *n.*, generation; age (325); years (508).

saepe, *adv.*, *compar.*, saepius, often.

saeta, -ae, *f.*, bristle.

saeviō (4), rage.

saevus, -a, -um, savage, dire.

sagitta, -ae, *f.*, arrow.

sagittifer, -era, -erum, arrow-bearing.

sagulum, -ī, *n.*, cloak.

Salamīs, -īnis, *f.*, Salamis (*island and town off coast of Attica, Greece*).

Saliī, -ōrum, *m. pl.*, the Salii (*priests of Mars*).

saltus, -ūs, *m.*, leap, bound.

salūs, -ūtis, *f.*, safety.

(salveō), -ēre (2), am well : *imperat.*, hail !

sānctus, -a, -um, holy.

sanguineus, -a, -um, bloody, blood-red.

sanguis, -inis, *m.*, blood.

saniēs, *in acc. and abl. sg. only, f.*, gore.

satis, *adv.*, enough.

Sāturnius, -a, -um, Saturnian.

Sāturnus, -ī, *m.*, Saturn.

saturō (1), fill.

satus, -a, -um, (*perf. part. of* sero), begotten (of), son (of).

saxeus, -a, -um, rocky.

saxum, -ī, *n.*, stone, rock, boulder.

scelus, -eris, *n.*, crime ; sin (668).

scēptrum, -ī, *n.*, sceptre.

scindō, -ere, scīdī, scissum (3), cut ; part (142) ; tear (702), divide.

scopulus, -ī, *m.*, rock, cliff, crag.

scūtum, -ī, *n.*, shield.

scyphus, -ī, *m.*, cup, goblet.

sē *or* sēsē, *gen.* suī, *reflex. pron. 3rd pers.*, himself, herself, itself, themselves.

secō, -āre, -uī, sectum (1), cut, cleave.

secrētus, -a, -um, withdrawn ; apart (610) ; *as neut. pl. noun*, seclusion (463).

secundus, -a, -um, second (283), favouring (302), following (545), heartening (90).

secus, *adv.*, otherwise.

sed, *conj.*, but.

sedeō, -ēre, sēdī, sessum (2), sit.

sēdēs, -is, *f.*, seat, dwelling, site.

sedīle, -is, *n.*, seat, site.

sēgnis, -e, slow ; idly (549).

sēmēsus, -a, -um, half-eaten.

sēmifer, -erī, *m.*, half-beast.

sēmihomo, -inis, *m.*, half-man ; *as adj.*, half-human.

semper, *adv.*, always.

senātus, -ūs, *m.*, senate,

senectūs, -ūtis, *f.*, old age.

senex, -is, *m.*, old man.

senior, *compar. adj. from* senex, old.

sentiō, -īre, sēnsī, sēnsum (4), feel, perceive, discern.

septēnī, -ae, -a, seven each (448) ; seven.

sequāx, -ācis, pursuing, vengeful.

sequor, -ī, secūtus (3), *dep.*, follow, favour.

serēnus, -a, -um, clear.

sermō, -ōnis, *m.*, converse.

serō, -ere, sēvī, satum (3), *lit.* sow, beget.

serpēns, -ntis, *f.*, snake, asp.

sērus, -a, -um, late, belated.

servō (1), keep, guard, preserve.

sēsē, *see* sē.

sevērus, -a, -um, stern.

sī, *conj.*, if.

sīc, *adv.*, thus, so.

Sīcanius, -a, -um, Sicanian = Sicilian.

Sicānus, -ī, *m.*, a Sicanian = Sicilian ; *also as adj.*

siccus, -a, -um, dry.

sīcut, *adv.*, just as.

sīdus, -eris, *n.*, constellation, star.

sīgnum, -ī, *n.*, sign ; track (212) ; standard (52, 498).

silex, -icis, *m. and f.*, flint.

silva, -ae, *f.*, wood, forest.

Silvānus, -ī, *m.*, Silvanus.

silvestris, -e, woodland.

similis, -e, like.

simul, *adv.*, at the same time ; *as conj.*, =simulac, as soon as.

sīn, *conj.*, but if.

sine, *prep. with abl.*, without.

singulī, -ae, -a, one by one.

sinus, -ūs, *m.*, bosom ; fold (712).

sistō, -ere, stitī, statum (3), place.

sīstrum, -ī, *n.*, a sistrum.

socius, -ī, *m.*, comrade, friend, ally ; *as adj.*, allied (120).

sōl, sōlis, *m.*, the sun.

sōlācium, -ī, *n.*, comfort, consolation, solace.

solitus, -a, -um, wonted, accustomed.

solium, -ī, *n.*, throne.

sollemnis, -e, wonted (102) ; *in neut. pl.*, solemn ceremonies.

solum, -ī, *n.*, soil, ground.

sōlus, -a, -um, only, sole.

solvō, -ere, -vī, solūtum (3), pay ; loosen (238).

somnus, -ī, *m.*, sleep, dream.

sonitus, -ūs, *m.*, sound ; thunder (525).

sopītus, -a, -um, slumbering.

sopor, -ōris, *m.*, sleep, slumber.

soror, -ōris, *f.*, sister.

sortior (4), *dep.*, apportion, share.

sospes, -itis, safe.

spargō, -ere, -rsī, -rsum (3), scatter, sprinkle.

spectō (1), look at, gaze ; try, test (151).

specus, -ūs, *m.*, cave, vault.

spēlunca, -ae, *f.*, cave.

spēs, speī, *f.*, hope.

spīrō (1), breathe.

spolium, -ī, *n.*, spoil.

spūmō (1), foam.

squāma, -ae, *f.*, scale.

stabulum, -ī, *n.*, stall, stable.

stāgnum, -ī, *n.*, pool.

statuō, -ere, -uī, -ūtum (3), set up.

sternō, -ere, strāvī, strātum (3), level (89) ; lay low (562, 566) ; strew (719).

Steropēs, -pis, *m.*, Steropes =
'Lightning', (*name of a Cy-clops*).

stirps, -is, *f.*, race ; breed (130).

stō, -āre, stetī, statum, (1) stand.

strātum, -ī, *m.*, couch, bed.

strepitus, -ūs, *m.*, noise, clamour.

strepō, -ere, -uī (3), blare (2).

strictūra, -ae, *f.*, mass *or* bar (*of metal*).

strīdeō (2), hiss.

strīdō (3), hiss.

stringō, -ere, strīnxī, strictum (3), skim (63).

struō, -ere, strūxī, strūctum (3), devise, plan.

stuppeus, -a, -um, of tow.

Stygius, -a, -um, Stygian, of the Styx.

sub, *prep. with acc. and abl.*, under ; up to (24).

subeō, -īre, -iī (īvī), -itum, enter (125, 363) ; draw near (359).

subigō, -ere, -ēgī, -āctum (3), compel, subdue.

subitō, *adv.*, suddenly.

subitus, -a, -um, sudden.

subiungō, -ere, -iūnxī, -iūnctum (3), subdue.

sublīgō (1), buckle ; fasten on.

subsistō, -ere, -stitī (3), halt.

subter, *adv., and prep. with acc.*, below.

subvehō, -ere, -vēxī, -vēctum (3), bear up *or* upwards.

succēdō, -ere, -cessī, -cessum (3), enter (123, 507) ; follow (327).

sūdum, -ī, *n.*, bright sky.

sum, esse, fuī, am.

summoveō, -ēre, -mōvī, -mōtum (2), remove ; *in perf. part. pass.*, remote, retired (193).

summus, -a, -um, highest, top of.

super, *adv., and prep. with acc.*, over, above.

superbus, -a, -um, proud, haughty.

superī, -ōrum, *m. pl.*, the gods above.

superō (1), overcome, conquer ; pass by (95) ; surpass (*intrans.*, 208).

superstitiō, -ōnis, *f.*, superstition.

supersum, -esse, -fuī, survive.

supplex, -icis, humble, suppliant.

supplicium, -ī, *n.*, punishment.

suprā, *adv. and prep. with acc.*, above.

suprēmus, -a, -um, highest ; last.

surgō, -ere, -rēxī, -rēctum (3), rise.

sūs, suis, *f.*, sow.

suscitō (1), rouse up ; awake (410).

suspendō, -ere, -pendī, -pēnsum (3), hang up.

suspiciō, -ere, -spēxī, -spectum, look upwards (527).

sustineō, -ēre, -tinuī, -tentum (2), support ; lift (70).

suus, -a, -um, *reflex. poss. adj.*, his, her, its, their own.

(tābum, -ī, *n., only in abl. sing.*, corruption.

tacitus, -a, -um, silent.

tālis, -e, such.

tam, *adv.*, so.

tamen, *adv.*, nevertheless.

tandem, *adv.*, at last ; I pray (73).

tantum, *adv.*, so much ; only (78).

tantus, -a, -um, so great.

Tarchō, -ōnis, *m.*, Tarcho.

tardus, -a, -um, slow ; sluggish (508).

Tarpēius, -a, -um, Tarpeian.

Tarquinius, -ī, *m.*, Tarquin.
Tartara, -ōrum, *n. pl.*, Tartarus (*the underworld*).
Tartareus, -a, -um, Tartarean.
Tatius, -ī, *m.*, Tatius (*a Sabine king*).
taurus, -ī, *m.*, bull.
tēctum, -ī, *n.*, roof, dwelling.
Tegeaeus, -a, -um, of Tegea (*in Arcadia, Greece*).
tegō, -ere, -xī, -ctum (3), cover ; overshadow (95).
tellus, -ūris, *f.*, earth.
tēlum, -ī, *n.*, missile, weapon.
templum, -ī, *n.*, temple.
temptāmentum, -ī, *n.*, a sounding, probing, (144).
temptō (1), try, essay.
tempus, -oris, *n.*, time ; *in pl.,* temples *of the head* (286, 680, 684).
tenāx, -ācis, tenacious, gripping.
tendō, -ere, tetendī, tentum *or* **tēnsum** (3), *lit.* stretch ; *in-trans.,* make one's way (113, 595) ; encamp (605).
tenebrae, -ārum, *f. pl.*, darkness, gloom.
teneō, -ēre, -uī, tentum (2), hold ; occupy (204).
tenuis, -e, thin, slender ; delicate (409).
tepeō (2), reek (196).
tepidus, -a, -um, warm.
ter, *adv.*, thrice.
teres, -etis, smooth.
tergeminus, -a, -um, triple.
tergum, -ī, *n.*, back ; chine (183) ; hide (460) ; **a tergo,** in rear, behind.
ternī, -ae, -a, three each, three ; triple (565).

terra, -ae, *f.*, earth, land.
terreō (2), terrify.
terribilis, -e, dreadful.
terrificus, -a, -um, frightful.
terror, -ōris, *m.*, dread, fright.
testor (1), *dep.,* bear witness to.
textum, -ī, *n.*, fabric.
Teucrī, -ōrum, *m. pl.*, the Trojans.
thalamus, -ī, *m.*, bed-chamber.
Thybris, -idis, *m.*, (1) the Tiber, (2) name of Italian chief from whom the river was named.
Tiberīnus, -ī, *m.*, Tiberinus (*the river god*) ; *as adj.,* of the Tiber
timeō (2), fear.
timor, -ōris, *m.*, fear.
tingō, -ere, -nxī, -nctum (3), dip.
Tirynthius, -a, -um, of Tiryns (*in Greece*).
Tithōnius, -a, -um, of Tithonus (*husband of Aurora*).
tolerō (1), endure, bear.
tollō, -ere, sustulī, sublātum (3), lift up, raise (452) ; hold on high (141) ; take away (175, 439).
tonitrus, -ūs, *m.*, thunder.
tonō, -āre, -uī, -itum (1), thunder.
tormentum, -ī, *n.*, torture.
torqueō, -ēre, torsī, tortum (2), twist.
torreō, -ēre, -uī, tostum (2), roast.
torus, -ī, *m.*, couch, bed.
tot, *indecl.*, so many.
totidem, *indecl.*, just so many.
tōtus, -a, -um, whole, entire.
trahō, -ere, trāxī, tractum (3), drag, draw.
trāns, *prep. with acc.*, across.
tremendus, -a, -um, dread.
tremō, -ere, -uī, (3), tremble at *or* before (297, 350, 669).

tremulus, -a, -um, quivering.

trepidō (1), tremble.

trepidus, -a, -um, alarmed ; hasty (5).

trēs, tria, three.

tridēns, -ntis, *lit.* three-toothed ; triple-pointed (690).

trīgintā, thirty.

triplex, -icis, triple.

trīstis, -e, sad ; ghastly (197) ; dreadful (701).

triumphus, -ī, *m.*, triumph.

Trōia, -ae, *f.*, Troy.

Trōiānus, -a, -um, Trojan.

Trōius, -a, -um, of Troy.

truncus, -ī, *m.*, tree-trunk.

tū, tuī, thou, you, *sg.* (*pl.* vōs).

tuba, -ae, *f.*, trumpet.

tueor (2), *dep.*, look at ; gaze upon (265).

Tullus, -ī, *m.*, Tullus Hostilius (*king of Rome*).

tum, *adv.*, then.

tumēns, -ntis, swelling.

tumidus, -a, -um, swelling.

tumor, -ōris, *m.*, swelling.

tumultus, -ūs, *m.*, rising (4) ; uprising (371).

tunica, -ae, *f.*, tunic.

turba, -ae, *f.*, throng, crowd.

turbō (1), stir, rouse (4) ; trouble (29, 223).

Turnus, -ī, *m.*, Turnus (*king of the Rutuli*).

turrītus, -a, -um, towered, turreted.

tūs, tūris, *n.*, incense.

Tuscus, -a, -um, Tuscan, Etruscan.

tūtus, -a, -um, safe.

tuus, -a, -um, thy, thine ; your.

Typhōeus, -eī, *m.*, Typhoeus (*a giant*).

tyrannus, -ī, *m.*, despot.

Tyrrhēnus, -a, -um, Tyrrhenian (=Tuscan).

ūber, -eris, *n.*, udder.

ubi, *adv. and conj.*, when.

Ufēns, -tis, *m.*, Ufens (*an Italian chieftain*).

ūllus, -a, -um, any.

ultimus, -a, -um, furthest.

ultor, -ōris, *m.*, avenger.

ultrō, *adv.*, beyond.

umbō, -ōnis, *m.*, boss (*of shield*).

umbra, -ae, *f.*, shade, shadow.

umbrōsus, -a, -um, shady.

umerus, -ī, *m.*, shoulder.

umquam, *adv.*, ever.

ūnā, *adv.*, together ; at the same time.

unda, -ae, *f.*, wave, water.

unde, *rel. adv.*, from which, from whom, whence.

undique, *adv.*, from *or* on all sides.

unguis, -is, *m.*, nail, claw.

ungula, -ae, *f.*, hoof.

ungō, -ere, unxī, ūnctum (3), caulk.

ūnus, -a, -um, one.

urbs, urbis, *f.*, city.

ursa, -ae, *f.*, she-bear.

usquam, *adv.*, anywhere.

ūsus, -ūs, *m.*, use, custom.

ut, *conj.*, (1) *with indic.*, when ; how (154) ; (2) *with subj.*, that, so that, in order that.

vādō, -ere (3), go.

vadum, -ī, *n.*, shoal, shallow.

valeō (2), am strong ; am able *or* avail (to).

validus, -a, -um, strong.

vallis, -is, *f.*, valley.

vānus, -a, -um, vain ; idle (187).

varius, -a, -um, diverse, various ; of divers kinds (95).

vāstō (1), lay waste ; strip (*with acc. and abl.*).

vāstus, -a, -um, vast, mighty.

vātēs, -is, *f.*, prophetess.

-ve, *conj.*, or.

vehō, -ere, vēxī, vēctum (3), draw.

vel, *conj.*, or.

vellō, -ere, vulsī, vulsum (3), pull down.

vēlō (1), veil.

vēlum, -ī, *n.*, sail ; **vēla dare**, to set sail.

velut, *adv.*, just as.

vēnātus, -ūs, *m.*, hunting, the chase.

veniō, -īre, vēnī, ventum (4), come.

ventōsus, -a, -um, windy, gusty.

ventus, -ī, *m.*, wind.

Venulus, -ī, *m.*, Venulus.

Venus, -eris, *f.*, Venus.

veprēs, -is, *m.*, bramble.

verbum, -ī, *n.*, word.

vērō, *adv.*, in truth.

verrō, -ere, vērrī, versum (3), sweep.

versō (1), turn (21, 453) ; handle (619).

vertex, -icis, *m.*, summit, top ; head (681).

vertō, -ere, -tī, -sum (3), turn.

vērus, -a, -um, true, real, genuine.

vescor, -ī (3), *dep.*, feed *or* feast upon.

Vesper, -erī *or* **-eris**, *m.*, the evening-star ; the west.

vester, -tra, -trum, your ; *as pron.*, yours.

vestīgium, -ī, *n.*, foot-print.

vestiō (4), clothe.

vestis, -is, *f.*, dress, garment ; raiment (712).

vetō, -āre, -uī, -itum (1), forbid.

vetus, -eris, old, ancient.

vetustus, -a, -um, old, ancient.

via, -ae, *f.*, way, path.

vibrō (1), *lit.* brandish ; **vibrātus fulgor**, a jagged flash of lightning.

victor, -ōris, *m.*, conqueror.

victus, -ūs, *m.*, way of life.

videō, -ēre, vīdī, vīsum (2), see ; *in pass.*, seem.

viduō (1), deprive, bereave.

villōsus, -a, -um, shaggy, rough.

vincō, -ere, vīcī, vīctum (3), conquer.

vinc(u)lum, -ī, *n.*, bond ; thong (458).

vīnum, -ī, *n.*, wine.

vir, virī, *m.*, man, hero.

virgātus, -a, -um, striped.

viridis, -e, green.

virtūs, -ūtis, *f.*, manliness, courage, merit.

vīs, *acc.* **vim**, *abl.* **vī**, *pl.*, **vīrēs, -ium**, *f.*, violence (243) ; *in pl.*, strength, might.

vīscera, -um, *n. pl.*, flesh (180) ; entrails (644).

vīsō, -ere, vīsī, vīsum (3), visit.

vīsus, -ūs, *m.*, sight.

vīta, -ae, *f.*, life.

vitta, -ae, *f.*, fillet, head-band.

vīvō, -ere, vīxī (3), live.

vīvus, -a, -um, living.

vix, *adv.*, scarcely, hardly.

vocō (1), call ; invoke (275)

volātilis, -e, winged, flying.

Volcānius, -ī, *n.*, of Vulcan.

Volcānus, -ī, *m.*, Vulcan.

volitō (1), flutter.

volō, velle, voluī, am willing, will, wish.

volō (1), fly.

volucer, -cris, -cre, winged ; flying, (433) ; *fem. sg. as noun*, bird.

voluptās, -tātis, *f.*, pleasure, delight.

volvō, -ere, -vī, -ūtum (3), roll.

vomō, -ere, -uī, -itum (3), belch forth, spout.

vōs, *pl.* of tū, you.

vōtum, -ī, *n.*, vow ; votive offering.

vōx, vōcis, *f.*, voice ; word.

vulgō (1), spread abroad, publish.

vulnerō (1), wound.

vulnificus, -a, -um, wounding.

vultus, -ūs, *m.*, face, countenance, features.

ADDITIONAL BIBLIOGRAPHY

Since this edition was first published in 1952, there has been a steady flow of scholarly work on the *Aeneid*. The student will find most useful W. A. Camps, *An Introduction to Virgil's Aeneid* (Oxford, 1969) and the excellent collection of essays in S. Commager (ed.) *Virgil: a Collection of Critical Essays* (Englewood Cliffs, 1966). Much work has been devoted to the appreciation of the *Aeneid* as literature, e.g. K. Quinn, *Virgil's Aeneid: a Critical Description* (London, 1968) and W. R. Johnson, *Darkness Visible* (Berkeley, 1976). The poem's unity has been sought vainly through structural analysis, e.g. G. E. Duckworth, *Structural Patterns and Proportions in Vergil's Aeneid* (Michigan, 1962); and with more success through the poet's imagery and symbolism, e.g. V Pöschl, *The Art of Vergil: Image and Symbol in the Aeneid* (Michigan, 1962) which maintains a reasonably balanced view, M. C. J. Putnam, *The Poetry of the Aeneid* (Cambridge, Mass., 1965) which is less restrained and often mistaken but does contain a chapter specifically on Book VIII, and J. W. Hunt, *Forms of Glory: Structure and Sense in Virgil's Aeneid* (Southern Illinois, 1973). Analysis of structure and imagery are linked with psychology (character) and with examination of underlying themes (e.g. the role of *fatum*, the opposition of *furor* and *pietas*) in B. Otis, *Virgil: a Study in Civilized Poetry* (Oxford, 1963). In the vein of more traditional scholarship Vergil's debt to earlier Roman poetry is examined by M. Wigodsky, *Vergil and Early Latin Poetry* (Wiesbaden, 1972) and his debt in Book VIII to Hellenistic Greek poetry by E. V. George, *Aeneid VIII and the Aitia of Callimachus* (Leiden, 1974). W. Warde Fowler's valuable essay on Book VIII, *Aeneas at the Site of Rome* (Oxford, 1917) has been reprinted along with his essays on Books VII and XII (New York, 1978); and two articles on particular sections of Book VIII may also prove useful: D. E. Eichholz 'The Shield of Aeneas' in *Proceedings of the Virgil Society* 6 (1966 - 7) 45 - 9 and G. K. Galinsky 'The Hercules-Cacus Episode in *Aeneid* VIII' in *American Journal of Philology* 87 (1966) 18 - 51. Two major books on Roman poetry in general should be mentioned: L. P. Wilkinson, *Golden Latin Artistry* (Cambridge, 1963) and G. Williams, *Tradition and Originality in Roman Poetry* (Oxford, 1968), whose abridged version, *The Nature of Roman Poetry* (Oxford, 1970) may prove most helpful to the student.

Further bibliography is provided by G. E. Duckworth, *Recent Work on Vergil* (1940 - 1956) (The Vergilian Society, 1964), by R. D. Williams, *Virgil: Greece and Rome Surveys in the Classics* (Oxford, 1967), and by R. G. Austin and R. D. Williams, *A Bibliography of Virgil* (J.A.C.T., 1978).